ONTARIO'S WILDLIFE

ONTARIO'S WILDLIFE

DAVE TAYLOR

THE
BOSTON MILLS
PRESS

To Anne,
who shared the adventure
and the frustration
and who never stopped supporting my dream.

Canadian Cataloguing in Publication Data

Taylor, J. David, 1948-
   Ontario's wildlife

Bibliography: p.
Includes index.
ISBN 0-919783-85-6

1. Zoology - Ontario. I. Title.

QL221.06T38   1988   591.9713   C88-094050-6

Published by:
THE BOSTON MILLS PRESS
132 Main Street
Erin, Ontario
N0B 1T0
(519) 833-2407
Fax: (519) 833-2195

American Association
for State and Local History
Award of Merit

Winners of the
Heritage Canada
Communications Award

Typography and Design by Lexigraf, Tottenham
Cover Design by Gill Stead, Guelph
Printed by Khai Wah Litho PTE Limited, Singapore

We wish to acknowledge the financial assistance of The Canada Council,
the Ontario Arts Council and the Office of the Secretary of State.

The photographs in this book were taken with Canon cameras and lenses.
I am grateful for this company's support. All of the slides were taken with
Kodachrome 64 film.

Contents

Black bear

Osprey

Massassauga rattlesnake

Chinook salmon

Painted turtle

ONTARIO

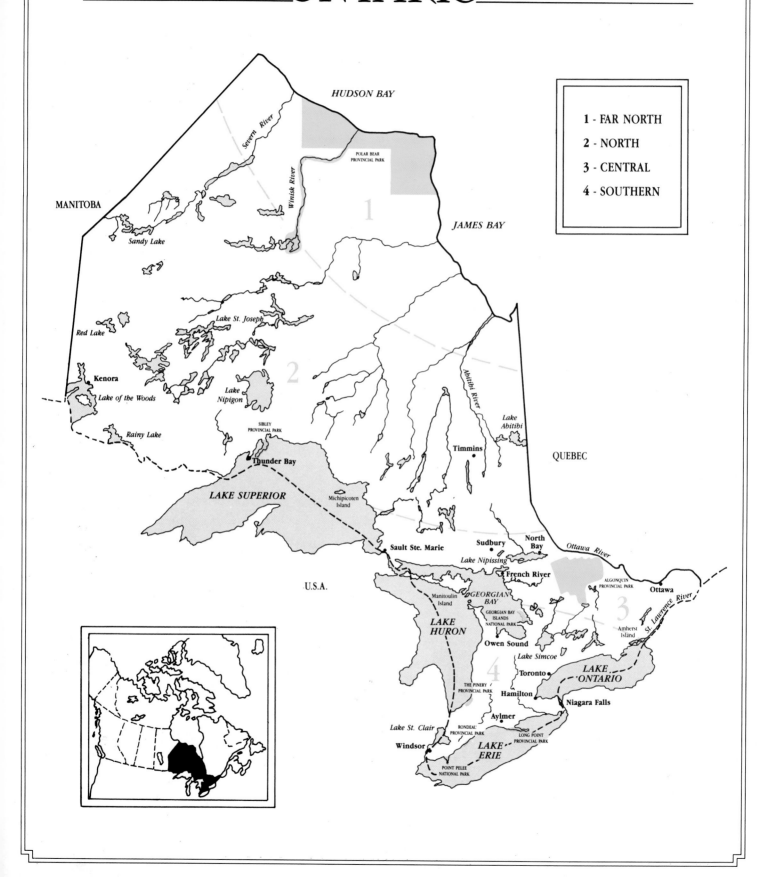

1 - FAR NORTH
2 - NORTH
3 - CENTRAL
4 - SOUTHERN

HUDSON BAY

Severn River

Winisk River

POLAR BEAR
PROVINCIAL PARK

JAMES BAY

MANITOBA

Sandy Lake

Lake St. Joseph

Red Lake

Kenora

Lake of the Woods

Lake Nipigon

Abitibi River

Lake Abitibi

QUEBEC

Rainy Lake

SIBLEY
PROVINCIAL PARK

Timmins

Thunder Bay

LAKE SUPERIOR

Michipicoten Island

Sault Ste. Marie

Sudbury

North Bay

Ottawa River

Lake Nipissing

French River

ALGONQUIN
PROVINCIAL PARK

Ottawa

U.S.A.

Manitoulin Island

GEORGIAN BAY

GEORGIAN BAY
ISLANDS
NATIONAL PARK

St. Lawrence River

Amherst Island

LAKE HURON

Owen Sound

Lake Simcoe

LAKE ONTARIO

4

Toronto

THE PINERY
PROVINCIAL PARK

Hamilton

Niagara Falls

Lake St. Clair

RONDEAU
PROVINCIAL PARK

Aylmer

LONG POINT
PROVINCIAL PARK

Windsor

LAKE ERIE

POINT PELEE
NATIONAL PARK

Introduction

Photo by Jim Markou

Dave Taylor is a teacher for the Peel Board of Education and a freelance writer and photographer specializing in natural history subjects.

He is a field editor for *Ontario Out of Doors* Magazine, where his work appears regularly. He also contributes to *Landmarks* magazine and a number of other publications across North America.

He is the author of *Game Animals of North America*.

Married with two daughters, he gets much enjoyment from sharing Ontario's outdoors with his family.

This book is for anyone who, like me, is interested in Ontario's wildlife. I've been fortunate enough to have stalked our province's various species from Point Pelee to Moosonee with a camera, and this book is the result of those experiences.

It is a personal book, for the most part. I've tried to combine in the text scientific research and my own experiences with each species. I've also tried to give the reader advice on where these animals can be seen and how they may be photographed.

This book contains only a few of the species found here. Over 400 species of birds occur within this province's boundaries along with nearly 80 species of mammals, 50 or so types of amphibians and reptiles, a large variety of fish and over 15,000 types of invertebrates.

To cover all of these would be an impossible task so this book has dealt with some of the more interesting species. Some, like the cougar, can best be viewed in zoos while others like the whitetailed deer are common throughout much of the province.

But don't let the text and the photographs fool you into thinking that photographing or even seeing our wildlife is easy. Yes, it is possible to see ten or more moose in a day of driving Algonquin's Highway 60, but the day begins at sunrise and ends at sunset! Yes, there are rivers where you can canoe past three osprey nests in an hour, but to get the accompanying pictures you must understand the bird's behaviour patterns and be willing to bake in the sun for a day.

Still, as you read this book, I hope you are struck by the richness and variety of wild creatures this province possesses. It is perhaps one of the best places in North America for a would-be wildlife photographer to live. At least I think so.

Black Bear

Black Bear
Ursus americanus

Height at shoulder: 3 to 3½ feet (91 to 107 cm)
Weight: 150 to 600 pounds (56 to 224 kg)
Range: All of the province except the southern portion, although even here occasional sightings occur.

Ask me which animal I have enjoyed photographing the most or which animal has given me some of my worst frights and I'll answer without pause. It has to be the black bear.

Over the years I've developed somewhat of a passion for photographing bears. Part of the reason is that they are predators, therefore less numerous and harder to find than non-predators like deer and moose. They are also more dangerous to work with, and that makes them more exciting. At the same time they are also more accommodating than other large predators, in that they can become habituated to people.

Their surroundings these days are not all that glamorous. If professional wildlife photographers are honest with you, they'll tell you that most bear pictures taken south of Alaska are of captive bears, bears in dumps or trained bears. Very few are of bears living in pristine wilderness. There are good reasons for this. Bears that are completely wild do one of two things when they come across people. Most often they vanish into the woods, something black bears are expert at. A very few bears choose option number two, and that is to view the person as a potential meal. These latter types, while rare, have accounted for a few killings each year in North America.

I've only been seriously threatened once by a black bear and that was due to my own foolishness. It was a dump bear that had just recently been in a fight. Cuts above its eye and on its nose attested to this and its growls gave me fair warning of its mood. Being young and foolish, I ignored the warnings and approached too close. A nearby car saved me from getting anything but badly scared!

Since then I've seen hundreds of bears, black and grizzly, and have suffered nothing more serious than a bluff charge. Indeed most black bears are very tolerant of human stupidity, and the typical black bear encounter usually has the bear either ignoring people or moving away from them. Not that anyone should ever take such an animal for granted. I always watch for any sign of tension on the bear's part and immediately back off if I see the animal becoming agitated.

Black bears are intelligent and well equipped for their environment. They have evolved behaviour strategies that make them far less aggressive than grizzly or polar bears. These bears, living on open tundra and Arctic ice fields, have found that aggression works best for them, but not the black bear. Given an option, it will vanish into the woods rather than fight. That applies to females with cubs too, unless you are so close that the mother feels truly threatened. Then watch out!

Black bears are excellent climbers as cubs and keep the skill throughout life. Adult bears will climb trees to get at fall masts of beechnuts, acorns, or other such goodies. Omnivores, they eat just about anything, including grass, nuts, berries, eggs, sedges, fruits and insects. They are also meateaters and recent studies in Alaska and Newfoundland have shown them to be significant predators of moose and caribou calves. They probably take whitetail fawns as well as moose calves in Ontario too.

To understand bears you have to understand their needs, which are simple: food. Bears have a digestive system about on par with a human's, which is to say it isn't very good. People consume food which is high in nutritional value in order to offset their poor digestive abilities. So do bears. In spring they will seek the first nourishing shoots of grass. Then, as other plants push out of the ground, the bears will move on to these.

Summer provides a feast of bear delights as blueberries, wild raspberries and other fruits ripen. One bear researcher averaged the number of berry seeds found in a bear's droppings and came up with a figure of 1,500. Given the number of piles in the area, that was one well-fed bear!

Another source of food in the summer is dumps. People food, even garbage, is more nutritious than most of a bear's natural food. Cooked food is even better! Always opportunists, bears are quick to utilize this potential food source, and it is here that most people see their first bear.

Bear-watching from the safety of your car can give you many insights into the bear's world. Two-year-old cubs, being low in the dominance hierarchy, are often the first to arrive and must feed at the most dangerous times. Often that means during daylight. Females with cubs are usually second to arrive, but the small cubs may not be visible, as they are often left up a tree while she feeds. Large dominant males feed when they decide to feed, usually well after dark. You may well see several bears feeding together peacefully, but as you continue to watch you will soon see who is boss.

Remember, should you go to the dump to see bears, that if you present a situation where there is potential for danger, it is the bear who ultimately loses. It will be shot. Stay in your car.

Bear cubs are shooed up trees when their mother goes off to feed or senses danger.

In the fall a bear will increase its weight by a quarter of its summer weight.

Polar Bear

Polar Bear
Thalarctos maritimus

Height at shoulder: 4 feet (122 cm)
Weight: 800 to 1,200 pounds (298 to 448 kg)
Range: The James Bay - Hudson Bay coastline.

I have never seen a wild polar bear in Ontario and probably never will.

The best and easiest place to see them is in Churchill, Manitoba, and without doubt I will one day travel there to add this species to my list. I include the animal in this book because so few people are even aware that it is an Ontario species.

Recent studies by the Ministry of Natural Resources along the Hudson Bay shore, and to a lesser extent James Bay, have produced some surprising figures. It was assumed for some time that Ontario might have less than 50 resident polar bears, but the data from the studies show that over 700 bears call Ontario home, although, being wanderers, they do not confine themselves solely to this province. Even more important is the evidence that their number is growing!

The polar bear is the most predatory of all bears and the most dangerous to man. Males feed almost exclusively on seals which abound on the ice of Hudson Bay. Females come ashore to den and give birth, and during lean times will feed on grass.

Only the female polar bear hibernates, and then for a much shorter period than do black bears. Black bears hibernate because they are deprived of their food sources during winter, but the polar bear's food source, seals, is available year-round, so there is no real need to sleep away part of the year. Female polar bears hibernate in order to give birth, which they do when the Arctic winter is fully on the land.

For the most part, females with cubs see few humans in Ontario. The Hudson Bay shoreline is muddy and treacherous and few canoeists venture there. Those that do would be wise to take precautions, for any wandering bear is almost certain to visit a camp, either out of curiosity or for food.

Over 700 polar bears call Ontario home.

Raccoon

Raccoon
Procyon lotor

Weight: 12 to 48 pounds (4.5 to 18 kg)
Range: Entire province except James Bay-Hudson Bay region.

A constant chirring sound finally disturbed my sleep and I awoke a bit unnerved by it. I was sleeping in a small pup tent, while my parents were in our larger tent with my sisters. They either hadn't heard the sound or weren't about to bother with it. That left it to me!

As soon as I crawled outside, it was evident that the dining tent was the location of the sounds. I knew what I'd find and sure enough, there, staring boldly into the beam of my flashlight, sat two large raccoons. That didn't surprise me so much as the fact that they had been able to unscrew the lid off of the peanut butter jar. There were days when I had trouble doing that!

A quick "shoo" and they were gone, only to return before I had climbed back into my sleeping bag. It was a sleepless night.

Raccoons, like black bears, are omnivores and will eat just about anything. They seem to favour wildlife found along the edges of streams and marshes, such as duck and turtle eggs, crayfish, frogs and clams. They also eat their fair share of plant material.

Like bears, they too are hibernators. As winter approaches they den up in some protected place to pass most of the winter away sleeping. The female will often hibernate with last year's offspring. This has survival value because of the shared warmth.

The once popular myth of hibernating animals sleeping the entire winter has been replaced by serious scientific fact. Some animals, like chipmunks, do go into a deep, almost deathlike sleep with low body temperatures and heart rates. Even these heavy sleepers can wake up, however, although it does take a while before they regain full consciousness. Raccoons and bears do not go into as deep a sleep and may wake up often during the winter.

Raccoons in particular are more active, especially during February and March, when the female will wake up during the night and go in search of a mate. She prowls the forest floor, vocally announcing her condition in the hopes that a male will join her. Once mated she returns to the den to sleep away a few more weeks of winter. The male returns to his den too until the next female calls to him.

An ideal time to see raccoons is during the late winter, when the days are warming. They like to climb to the top branches of their tree and sun themselves. Try going out on a warm, sunny, early spring day and you will almost certainly see a few of these sunbathers.

For last year's young the warming days mean that mother will chase them away as she prepares to give birth to as many as four or five babies. About six to eight weeks after birth these new arrivals will join their mother on her nightly foraging and will be able to feed themselves.

Raccoons are opportunists and will den anywhere they feel safe. This includes hollow trees, caves, culverts, under buildings and even chimneys. They are a major annoyance in some Ontario cities, for once they take up residence in a chimney they can be hard house guests to get rid of. Smoking them out often results in their death, leaving their bodies wedged in the chimney to rot — not at all a pleasant situation for the house owner.

A much better solution is to wait until the family is out foraging and then cap the chimney. Better still, call for a professional pest controller.

Raccoons quickly learn to frequent places where people leave out food in garbage pails or where people provide food especially for them. They do carry a variety of diseases, including rabies, and while they may make attractive night visitors, it is not a good idea to encourage hand feeding.

In Ontario it is illegal to keep as a pet any native wild species without written permission (rarely given) from the Ministry of Natural Resources. However, many humane societies will rescue orphaned baby raccoons and look for volunteers to raise them until the fall. You may wish to contact your local humane society if this appeals to you. After the summer the males do get belligerent and you will likely be glad to see them go.

Moose

Moose
Alces alces

Height at shoulder: 6 to 7 feet (183 to 213 cm)
Weight: male, 900 to 1,400 pounds (336 to 522 kg) female, 700 to 1,100 pounds (261 to 410 kg)
Antler spread: 4 to 5 feet (122 to 152 cm)
Range: Northern mixed and boreal forests throughout the province. Absent only from farmlands and large urban areas.

The bull moose is the largest member of the deer family. This fact was never more obvious to me than the time I found myself face to face with one in the Algonquin Park bush. A friend and I had heard the moaning of a cow moose as she called to her mate and we had rather noisily stalked her. In the past our awkwardness at dragging telephoto lenses on tripods through the tangled underbrush had invariably caused a hasty retreat by our subjects. Not this time!

When we emerged into the relative openness of the forest, we found ourselves face to face with a cow, her calf and her would-be lover. None showed any inclination to flee, and we became spectators to the rut of the moose. As with all of Ontario's deer, the rut or mating season for moose is in the fall. Because of the vast expanse of forest in which they live, moose have a hard time finding each other. Visibility is poor in these surroundings, so moose locate potential mates by sound.

Cow moose are very vocal. On almost any late September night, if you take a quiet stroll away from your campfire and listen carefully, you will sooner or later hear the distant bawl of a cow moose. The bull moose hears it too and will seek out the cow, who could be as far away as a mile or more!

Then begins the courting, which leaves the bull confused and bewildered. The cow wants him but at the same time rejects his advances, deciding the time and the place mating will occur. At least that's what's supposed to happen.

In our case the bull must have been too successful during the night, for he chased the cow away a couple of times when she nuzzled him. Then she lay down and we made our first mistake. We got too close to her and he charged, intent on protecting his mate from other suitors!

A six-foot, 1,000-pound lovesick bull moose is not something to toy with. We ran, all cameras and tripods, flailing away at saplings and vines, until he stopped. Then the dangerous game began again. Finally, I charged him. A bluff but a noisy one! He ran for a bit and then stopped to stare at me. After that a truce existed and for three hours we photographed this rare trio before they finally retreated into the darkness of the pine forest.

Let me point out that I do not recommend such close contact with moose. They are dangerous animals in the fall. And they are not easy to photograph. In fact in 18 years of photographing them, these were easily my most co-operative subjects.

Should you wish to see moose first-hand, I'd advise a trip up to Algonquin Park in May or June. Moose are everywhere! In one day it is not unusual to see ten along Highway 60. The moose come there to lick the winter road salt from pools of meltwater beside the road. A slow drive through the park will almost guarantee a sighting.

Summer is almost as good because there are so many moose in the park that some are always near the road. Early morning or late evening are best, but I've seen them at all times of the day. I've also seen the results of moose and car accidents that happen at night. It's rough on the car and almost always fatal to the moose. Sometimes it's fatal to the driver too. Drive slowly from dusk to dawn.

For a truly remarkable moose encounter, take one of the park's many canoe routes. Few canoeists leave without seeing a moose and many get close-up views as the moose continue feeding as the canoe glides by.

Moose can also be seen in the spring along most northern highways. Sibley Provincial Park is also a good place to view moose in the summer, but not nearly as good as Algonquin Park.

A calf stays close to its mother during its first year.

A bull courts a cow moose in Algonquin Park.

Whitetail Deer

Whitetail Deer
Odecoileus virginianus

Height at shoulder: 3 to 3½ feet (91 to 107 cm)
Weight: 75 to 300 pounds (28 to 112 kg)
Range: The southern two thirds of the province but most common in agricultural areas.

The history of the whitetail deer in Ontario illustrates how the coming of the Europeans influenced the province's wildlife.

There is a myth that when the white man arrived on this continent the whitetail population was not very high compared to today's population. The myth goes that, as farmland replaced forest it opened up the edge habitat, where field and forest meet, that is ideal for deer. Recent research suggests, however, that North America's pre-settler deer population was in the range of 30 to 40 million, as compared to the 15 or 16 million that exist today.

A sudden reduction of the whitetail population occurred as the Europeans moved westward, dropping the population to around 2 or 3 million animals. Then, in the early 1800s, the whitetail rebounded, finally taking advantage of the agricultural land opened up to them. This rebound was of short duration, ending with the arrival of repeating rifles and the renewed westward expansion following the Civil War.

Ontario was poor deer range at best until the land was cleared. The logging techniques employed in the latter half of the 1800s provided suitable land and the deer moved north, extending their range into the Huntsville-Algonquin Park region. Market-hunting became popular in southern Ontario around this time, and by the beginning

The most popular big game animal in Ontario is the whitetail deer.

of this century, whitetail deer were almost extinct in the southern regions. Things were so bad in the South that Rondeau Provincial Park, when it was created in 1894, imported seven deer, which were then kept in a display pen. There were no wild deer left there!

Travellers in the Parry Sound area today may well see period hunting camp pictures, from the 1890s to the 1920s, showing hunters with large numbers of deer draped in front of their tents. This was the heyday of these camps, when deer flourished in newly opened forests and hunting regulations were scant.

Declining deer herds led to the creation of hunting seasons and deer limits. It also brought about the demise of many a predator, as the bounty system encouraged the killing of any "bad" animals (like wolves) that ate the "good" deer. Of course we now recognize that this was based on the notion that it was okay for mankind to kill deer but heaven help anything else that did! Today biologists and game managers recognize the rights and needs of both predators (human and otherwise) and prey when formulating management strategies.

As the deer numbers climbed again in the southern parts of the province, they also climbed in the North. This had some very serious effects on the moose population. Deer carry a brain worm which in no way affects their health. Eventually the larvae of the worm pass out of their host in its droppings. Should they find themselves released into marshes, the larvae cling to the underside of water plants, where they await the arrival of a new host animal, who will swallow them and allow them to complete their life cycle. If that animal is a moose, then death is the ultimate result. The worms, which do not bother deer, are deadly to moose, and it is not long before the deer herd replaces the moose herd in such areas.

Visitors to Algonquin Park in the 1950s tell of seeing 20 or 30 deer along the road, but no moose. In the 1960s deer were less common and in the 70s they were all but gone. The cry went up blaming the park's wolves, but they were more or less innocent. Better forest fire fighting techniques and stricter logging restrictions in the park meant that Algonquin's forest was returning to its old self. It was growing up and out of reach of the deer herd.

Algonquin was marginal deer range at best and these changes, coupled with a few severe winters, knocked the deer population down to a point from which it has never recovered. The moose were quick to respond and now number over 3,000 animals.

The other animal that suffered was the park's wolves. They could hunt deer but they had little knowledge about moose, having had so few to hunt for decades. The wolf population tumbled and is only now recovering.

Don't feel badly for the deer. In the South their numbers have skyrocketed. Rondeau now has a resident herd of over 400, and in the fall an estimated 800 seek refuge there during the hunting season.

Much of Ontario's success with deer has to do with new hunting laws that encourage the taking of antlerless deer. This policy provides more hunting revenue for deer management and also gives males a better chance of surviving to pass on their genes. Since 1980 the province's deer population has doubled and may be able to increase by as much again!

In marginal areas to the north, deer studies have indicated that deer may need to be fed if the snow exceeds certain depths. Researchers have also found out that the crucial times for deer are the months of December and March. They have evolved eating habits that allow them to survive the worst of winter but need help going into and coming out of the season. This help is provided by local conservation groups. Wolves too are monitored and are controlled if they put undue pressure on the deer herd.

Should you wish to see deer, they are present in many provincial parks, but the best areas are Rondeau and The Pinery provincial parks. They are very common throughout all of southern Ontario, however.

During the fall, rutting bucks are very aggressive animals.

The spots on this fawn are excellent camouflage.

By fall the fawn has lost its spots and looks like a miniature of its mother.

Elk

Elk
Cervus canadensis

Height at shoulder: 4½ to 5 feet (137 to 152 cm)
Weight: 450 to 1,100 pounds (168 to 410 kg)
Range: Confined to the Burwash area south of Sudbury.

Elk were never abundant in the province and by the 1800s they were gone. They were an animal that required grasslands and Ontario provided only a few suitable areas, most of them not far from the present site of Windsor.

There have been attempts to return elk, captured in the West, to the province, but most ended in failure. A few may still survive north of Lake Huron in the Chapleau Game Reserve and possibly in other spots, but their existence remains in doubt. At least it does in all but one spot. There is no doubt that some elk survive in the Burwash-French River area south of Sudbury. These elk are descendants of a herd released here in 1933. They were kept in a large fenced enclosure on the site of the Burwash Prison farm.

Sharing this pen was a herd of bison, and these animals were quite capable of knocking the fence down, which they did. Soon both elk and bison took up a free-ranging lifestyle. Today the bison are gone, but the elk have survived despite attempts in the 1950s to eliminate them because they were thought to pose a health problem. Estimates of their current number range up to 150 animals.

Elk have been reported all along the Georgian Bay coast, from Parry Sound to Sudbury, but most sightings centre around the islands at the mouth of the French River.

I wish I could say I've seen elk in this province, but I can't. I have spent weeks photographing them in the West, however, and have come to appreciate them as truly remarkable members of the deer family.

Late September is the time to be in elk country, for it is their rut. Rut is derived from a latin word meaning roar.

It describes the sound male members of the deer and cattle family make when they are in their breeding season. "Roar" however doesn't really describe the sound an elk makes, for it is more like a bugle.

To hear this sound echo off distant hills is to hear one of nature's great sounds (right up there with the cry of loons and the howl of wolves). It is a bull's way of warning other males that he is about. If he has cows in his harem, it challenges other males to stay away or fight. If he doesn't, it tells the cows where he is so they may seek him out.

When rival bulls meet, their huge antlers are put to their main purpose. Antlers, unlike horns, are regrown each year and serve as advertisements of a male's virility. The bigger they are, the healthier he is!

Only when males of equal size meet over a cow herd will they fight, locking antlers as they shove each other to and fro to determine who is the stronger. These battles are over quickly, but they are one of the most exciting sequences a wildlife photographer can hope to record.

Your best chances of seeing such sights are out west, but the Metro Toronto Zoo and the Montsburg Conservation Area near Guelph both have captive herds that may give you some feeling of the animal's majesty.

Elk are also ranched around the province to meet the demand in the Far East for fresh antlers as an aphrodisiac, and elk meat is served in some restaurants. These "game ranches" are taking the pressure off wild populations and are helping preserve them.

Bull elk of equal size fight to determine breeding success.

A bull elk performs a lip curl or flehem during the fall rut.

A calf elk nuzzles its mother.

Caribou

Caribou
Rangifer tarandus

Height at shoulder: 3 to 3½ feet (91 to 107 cm)
Weight: 150 to 600 pounds (56 to 224 kg)
Range: The northwestern third of the province.

The provinces to both the east and west of Ontario boast much larger herds of caribou than does Ontario. In fact Quebec is home to the largest single caribou herd in North America. The Ungava herd numbers over half a million animals, while Ontario's herd likely wouldn't total a tenth of that number, although precise estimates are hard to come by. One thing does seem certain: caribou numbers across the Arctic are on the upswing after decades of decline. The Ontario Ministry of Natural Resources is undertaking new research programs which will confirm whether this trend is also occurring here.

Ontario caribou are a subspecies known as woodland caribou. The name describes their forest habitat.

The great herds further north migrate onto the tundra, where large quantities of food are available to them. At these times, huge grazing herds drift across the open land in one of the last great spectacles of animal migrations on Earth. These herds break up as they return to their wintering grounds south of the treeline.

Ontario's caribou don't migrate to the tundra but instead stay within the boreal forest year-round. Here their chosen food, lichen, is harder to come by and the caribou are found in small bands of around 20 animals. These smaller herds reduce competition for the available food. They also make the caribou much harder to find, count and study.

Within historical times caribou were found as far south as Algonquin Park, but today are found only north of Lake Superior. The only exception to this is a small herd that lives on some islands in the lake itself.

Canoeists in some of the northern provincial parks may see caribou on rare occasions, but for the rest of us the chance of seeing these animals is, for the time being, most unlikely.

Caribou appear to be making a comeback in Ontario.

Wolf

Wolf
Canis lupus

Height at shoulder: 26 to 38 inches (66 to 96.5 cm)
Weight: 50 to 130 pounds (19 to 48.5 kg)
Range: All of province except southern Ontario.

Almost no one in the province is neutral about wolves. Some hate the species and point to the damage they do to deer herds, while others argue that they represent a wonderful species and admire the wolf's intelligence and devotion to family.

Neither attitude presents a fair picture of the wolf. Like all species it has a role to play in the province's ecology, and to judge it in human terms as being a crazed killer or a doting parent is to impose values on it that the wolf does not possess.

Wolves are predators. They do kill for a living, but like almost all members of the dog family, they are not very efficient killers when it comes to large prey. Unlike large cats, who often succeed in killing their prey instantly by breaking their necks, wild dogs often end up feeding on their prey while it is still alive. To human eyes it is an ugly and violent death, but to the wolf it is survival.

They can have a severe impact on northern deer herds, especially during harsh winters. It should be remembered that this is partly because the deer are at the extreme end of their range and are poorly equipped to handle the extra danger posed by wolves. Other prey species, such as moose, beaver and the smaller animals, take this danger in stride.

Recent studies have shown that prey species such as moose can actually control wolf numbers rather than the other way around. A healthy moose population has little to fear from wolves, and it is only when moose are too numerous for their food supply that wolves can really lower their numbers. Then a period of high wolf population results for a year or two. These extra wolves soon die off once the number of moose has returned to a better balance between its numbers and available food.

For most of the year, except winter, wolves feed on much smaller wildlife, including mice, voles, lemmings, birds, beaver and the occasional fox. Fox, perhaps because they are competition for the wolf, are not tolerated and are killed and eaten whenever the opportunity presents itself.

Wolves are among the best of nature's parents, although only the dominant pair in the pack breed. Other pack members share in raising the young and looking after them. Despite this, few young survive their first winter. As with most young wild animals, wolf cubs are often surplus animals who lack the experience to cope with hunters and trappers or to compete successfully for food. Those that do survive their first year usually pick up enough experience to survive for some time to come.

The howling of wolves is a thrill to hear and one of the best examples of animal communication known. Wolves sing or howl for many reasons. Often it is to help locate each other. This is the type of howl you can try to imitate in places like Algonquin, where wolves are common and close to the highway several times during the summer. A low, deep, mournful cry rising to the familiar tremor may very well bring results. The deeper howls are those of adult males, while the yapping, higher-pitched ones belong to the pups. Sometimes it seems they howl just for the sheer joy of it.

Wolves will also howl in response to other sounds. One night years ago, when I was a teenager working in Algonquin Park, I had to wait for my ride to pick me up at the junction of the Rock Lake Road and Highway 60. It was late and the traffic was light, so I started to sing to help keep back the imposing darkness. Suddenly I was joined by the howling of a wolf pack. I knew they posed no threat because there are, even today, only a very few documented cases of wolves attacking people. I stopped singing and listened to their chorus. Soon they too stopped, and after a few minutes I began to sing again.

A sound, half heard over my own voice, stopped me cold. I listened and could make out the sound of scratching on the road. I could also hear the sounds of something moving through the bushes behind me. Suddenly all my confidence in what I ''knew'' about wolves was gone, and I grabbed a stick and waited . . .

Then I was alone. A check next day showed wolf tracks all around the place I'd stood. It was a night I'll always remember and since then wolves have always been special to me.

The howling of wolves is one of the most stirring sounds to be heard in Ontario's wilderness.

Wolves come in a variety of colours from white through to black. This wolf is typical of the wolves found in Algonquin Park.

Coyote

Coyote
Canis latrans

Height at shoulder: 23 to 26 inches (58 to 66 cm)
Weight: 20 to 40 pounds (7.5 to 15 kg)
*Range: Entire province except the extreme northern James Bay-
Hudson Bay region. It is most common where wolves are absent.*

Coyotes are perhaps better known in this province as brush wolves. The name fits them because they are in fact a small wolf and they do seem to prefer brush more than they do the province's forests.

They are one of the true wildlife success stories on the continent. Despite being branded as vermin and destroyed by every possible means, including hunting (from planes, snowmobiles and horseback), trapping, the gassing and dynamiting of den sites, and wholesale poisoning campaigns, they have thrived.

The range of the coyote, once the western third of the continent south of Alaska, the Yukon and the Northwest Territories, now includes the whole continent. In Ontario they are believed to have arrived in two waves. The first came across from the Manitoba border into the north-western portion of the province, while the second crossed over from New York State and Michigan. Since then they have blended into one population, the members of which are slightly heavier on average than their western counterparts.

The coyote was able to do this by taking advantage of its bigger relative's demise. As the wolf was hunted out, the coyote moved in. It was smaller and could therefore survive on smaller prey than could the wolf. More importantly, it could tolerate and even exploit people and the environment they created, where the wolf couldn't.

I live in Mississauga, a fairly urban environment, yet I see coyotes fairly regularly on my travels. An excellent spot is the Pearson International Airport, where I've seen as many as five at one time. I've found dens along the river valleys near my home and once nearly hit a coyote on the 401 highway at Erin Mills Parkway.

A friend of mine who lives not far from the east end of Toronto regularly has coyotes court his two female dogs when they come into heat, while another friend hears and sees them on his drive in to work from Guelph.

Coyotes or brush wolves have shown that they can live quite close to people without being a pest or a hazard. Some however are tempted by lamb chops and chicken wings and turn to killing livestock. Each year a few cases are reported from around the province where coyotes have killed large numbers of sheep, pigs or chickens. Then highly trained trappers are called in to deal with them. It is apparently not difficult to trap young coyotes. Their wiser parents, however, are another matter. They survived by learning how to avoid traps and baits, and present a challenge few trappers are equal to. Once these experienced animals are dealt with, it may be years before coyotes return to an area.

Coyotes do perform some valuable services, however. They eat many of the animals which damage a farmer's crop, such as mice and blackbirds, and they keep fox numbers down. When coyotes move in, foxes move out or they are killed. This is a major benefit to both people and livestock because fox are a major carrier of rabies and are responsible for the spread of the disease to cattle, sheep, horses, other wildlife and people. Few if any coyotes carry or spread disease, and by removing foxes they help control this deadly disease.

For me, they are an intriguing and difficult species to photograph. I've certainly seen them often enough around the province, but they've never been too co-operative. Out west, however, I've found some of them to be regular hams who seem to delight in posing for the camera.

Coyotes are now an established member of Ontario's fauna, and they are common, as predators go, particularly in protected areas where hunting is not allowed. Good areas to look for them include urban areas where farmlands and river valleys still intrude. Winter is the best time to see them, for they will often hunt during the day. Look for a set of fresh tracks and then follow them, using binoculars to check out fence rows. Coyotes will often rest by these, and as you approach they will either bolt or sneak away.

If you start watching local fields, you will sooner or later see one — though most passers-by dismiss the coyote as a farmer's dog out for a run and drive on unaware that they have just seen a true survivor!

The coyote is better known in Ontario as the brush wolf.

*Coyote pups will stay with their parents and may even help
raise the next year's generation.*

Red Fox

Red Fox
Vulpes vulpes

Height at shoulder: 15 to 16 inches (38 to 41 cm)
Weight: 7 to 15 pounds (3 to 6 kg)
Range: The entire province.

Of all the members of the dog family found in this province, the fox is the most cat-like. While both wolves and coyotes will hunt in packs, the fox, like the wild cats, is a solitary hunter. Its pupils are slits like the cats' (all the better to see at night) and even its tracks are cat-like. Except for the telltale claw marks that cat tracks lack, fox tracks could easily be mistaken for a feline's.

There are three species of fox found within our borders. To the north, along the coast of James and Hudson bays, is the range of the Arctic fox. They roam over large areas and often follow polar bears out onto the pack ice, feeding on the scraps of their kills. At the extreme southern end of the province, a few grey foxes may be found. (The Ministry of Natural Resources reports that a few are trapped each decade, but are not certain whether the animals actually breed here or merely wander across the border from the United States.)

The red fox, however, calls the entire province home. As winter comes to an end, the female fox begins to search for a den where she will give birth to four to eight kits.

The kits will remain at one of several den sites until August, when the family will disperse. Radio-collared males have been known to travel over 150 miles from where they were born. Females don't travel as much, but they do cover some distances.

Because the red fox is a carrier of rabies, this dispersal pattern presents a major concern to wildlife biologists. Rabies, while always fatal, can remain dormant for several months. If the kits' mother is infected, she will give the disease to her kits, who could then carry it great distances. For example, a kit born on the Bruce Peninsula in spring could wind up carrying the disease to a pet cat as far away as Toronto the following December.

The Ministry of Natural Resources is hoping that a newly developed air-dropped oral rabies vaccine will help control the spread of this disease and perhaps even eliminate it from the province. Their studies so far indicate that foxes will take these packets dropped from the sky, and the chances for success look good.

Even though it may pose a potential health hazard, the red fox remains an animal worthy of our interest, just be wary of any fox seen lingering about and use some common sense when watching it.

Both parents help with the feeding of the cubs once they are weaned, bringing back to the den rabbits, chipmunks and other small prey. I've found deer legs at fox dens on a few occasions, but these must have been scavenged, probably from road kills, as the fox is too small to bring down a deer.

Foxes, being omnivorous, don't confine their eating habits to meat and fowl. Nuts, seeds, sedges, berries, wild grapes, insects and anything else that suits their fancy is consumed with relish. Some have even become roadside beggars, feeding on handouts of bread and bits of apples.

Over the years the red fox has provided me with some of my most remarkable experiences as a wildlife photographer. Usually once a fox is spotted, they quickly take off for parts unknown, but more than once they have continued hunting, completely ignoring my presence.

The most remarkable of my encounters with wild foxes happened a few years ago in Algonquin Park. My brother-in-law and I were up there one May weekend to photograph moose when shortly after noon we saw a red fox trotting along Highway 60, her mouth crammed full with three or four chipmunks. We got out of the car and followed her until we lost her in some brush by a sandbank. We'd almost given up when we heard a sound and then saw her staring at us. We quickly clambered up the bank, ignoring the hundreds of blackflies that had by now discovered us. Of course the noise we made caused the fox to disappear, and we were set to leave when once more she appeared, about ten feet away. This time she lay down and was soon joined by two dark-coloured kits, whom she proceeded to nurse.

I don't expect that will ever happen again, but with red foxes I've learned that almost anything is possible.

Cougar

Cougar
Felis concolor

Weight: 75 to 275 pounds (28 to 103 kg)
Range: The Ottawa Valley in the east and around Lake Superior and the Lake of the Woods. Very spotty distribution.

Does it or doesn't it exist in Ontario? That's the question most often asked about this cat. Once assumed extirpated from the province, a nagging series of sightings of long-tailed cats about the size of collies began showing up in Ministry of Natural Resources documents in the late 1950s. And they continue today.

What is this mystery animal? There is no doubt that the cat in question is a cougar, but that doesn't answer the question. You see, it could be a western cougar, in which case it is probably either a cat that was released when its owner realized that something that could eat you didn't make a great pet, or it is an escapee from someone's private zoo.

Or it could be an eastern cougar. The eastern cougar was a subspecies that used to live in the eastern third of the continent. The last known one was shot here early in this century and the species was presumed lost to the world. However, as deer rebounded from their brush with extinction, cougar sightings began to increase all over the East. Had the eastern cougar somehow managed to survive, or were they "escapees"?

No one really knows for sure, but it does seem quite likely that somehow the eastern cougar survived in small isolated pockets. Ontario now has the cougar on its endangered species list, which gives it full protection.

If you see one, report the sighting immediately. So far not even tracks or hair samples have been found confirming its existence. The mystery will only be solved once one of these animals can be photographed or examined by trained wildlife biologists.

Most sightings have been from around the north shore of Lake Superior and the Ottawa Valley. Sightings on the Bruce and in the area around Brantford are almost certainly released "western" cats. Sightings around Lake of the Woods could be eastern cougars but may also be western cougars expanding their range eastward.

The eastern cougar, once thought to be extinct, seems to be holding on in small numbers throughout the province.

Bobcat

Bobcat
Lynx rufus

Weight: 15 to 35 pounds (6 to 13 kg)
Range: Very local in range but found around Lake of the Woods, Lake Superior, the southeastern part of the province, and possibly locally in other pockets.

The bobcat at first glance appears to be a smaller version of the lynx. It is really almost the same size. The illusion is due to the bobcat's shorter legs in relation to its body size. Lynx have much longer legs and wider paws than do their close relatives.

The lynx is a creature of deep snow and needs its longer legs to move about during Ontario's winters. Bobcats evolved to suit winters further south, where they could get by without such aids. This difference between the two cats explains the reason for the bobcat's scarcity throughout the province. Quite simply, they aren't built for Ontario's climate.

Still they are common, as predators go, in two spots: the Lake of the Woods region in the West and the Blind River — Espanola portion of central Ontario. Here a few are trapped each year, confirming the existence of a breeding population.

Their food consists of small mammals and birds, with an occasional deer thrown in for good measure. They seem to do little damage to the number of prey animals in an area, and indeed most people are probably totally unaware of the cat's presence.

Every now and again I hear of bobcat sightings in southern Ontario, especially along the Bruce Peninsula and the Niagara Escarpment, but whether these are sightings of bobcats or pet cats gone wild is hard to determine.

If you should see one of these cats, count yourself very lucky indeed.

The bobcat is found only in a few isolated pockets in Ontario.

Lynx numbers go in cycles that coincide with the rise and fall of snowshoe hare numbers.

Snowshoe hares change from brown to white as winter approaches.

Canada Lynx

Canada Lynx
Lynx canadensis

Weight: 10 to 40 pounds (4 to 15 kg)
Range: All but the southern portion of the province, from the Ottawa Valley west to Windsor.

Lynx were once the subject of one of the North's great mysteries. What happened to them that made them disappear every six or seven years?

For centuries trappers would find lynx in large numbers one year and then hardly a one the next. Overtrapped? Possibly, but why the growing number of lynx in years following these sudden drops when trapping did not let up?

It wasn't until early this century that an Ontario researcher thought to check the trapping records of the Hudson's Bay Company and discovered a major clue to the mystery. He noted that the numbers of snowshoe hare trapped always peaked the year before the number of lynx trapped peaked. When he plotted them on a line graph, the lynx numbers rose and fell in a similar pattern to that of the snowshoe hare, only one year later. The solution? The hares did it!

At least that's what everyone believed. The theory went that as the hare's numbers increased, so too did the lynx's. More lynx meant more hares being eaten, and this led to the sudden decline of snowshoe hare numbers. With no food left, the lynx, so the theory went, died off the next year. A great theory linking predator to prey, but it let the real culprit off the hook.

It wasn't until the 1930s that another Ontario

Lynx are well suited for Ontario's winters.

student, Duncan MacLuich, working on his doctorate, decided to verify the lynx-hare relationship. He discovered that it was the hare's food, mostly woody browse, that was the real cause of the snowshoe's misfortune.

What happened was this. When snowshoe numbers were low, the shrubs and bushes that they fed on were more than healthy enough to outgrow the hare's browsing. Good food equalled healthy hares, which in turn gave them an edge over the lynx, meaning more hares survived. But as the hare's numbers increased, so did the lynx's. At the same time, the hares began to overeat the shrubs and this caused a remarkable response from the shrubs. In order to discourage hares from feeding on them, the plants produced bark and leaves that were less nourishing. The chemical content of the plants even inhibited the reproductive organs of the female snowshoes.

Fewer babies caused the population to suddenly crash, leaving the lynx without their normal food source, and they crashed too. Then the cycle repeated itself.

Trappers and wildlife managers now keep careful records on both species and when the crash comes all lynx trapping ceases in that area for two or three years. This careful policy should insure that lynx will be around for some years to come.

That doesn't mean that they will be easy to see, for like all cats they are secretive, and lynx more than others steer clear of humans. You might possibly hear one, however. Should you be out in the wilderness one summer night and hear cries of such anguish and terror that they send chills up your spine, you most likely will have heard the mating call of these cats. Throw another log on the fire, get close to someone and hope that that's what the sound is.

A young cottontail has many enemies to avoid if it is to survive.

Cottontail rabbits use deep snow as a blanket for both warmth and protection.

Cottontail

Cottontail
Sylvilagus floridanus

Weight: 2 to 4½ pounds (1 to 2 kg)
Range: The southern region of the province.

When the first settlers came to Ontario in 1786, they would not have found an animal that today is taken for granted in the southern portion of the province: the cottontail rabbit.

There was no recorded specimen of this rabbit here until one was killed near Windsor in 1886, though there have been cottontail bones found in archaeological sites dating back before the arrival of the Europeans. Did the early settlers miss this species? It seems unlikely, as biological surveys from the time were pretty thorough. I suspect that the answer lies in climatic changes.

Over the last few hundred years Ontario's climate has fluctuated. There have been colder decades and warmer ones. It is possible that the province's cottontail population ebbed and flowed with these climatic fluctuations.

Cottontails are a "carolinian" species. They prefer a milder climate where a habitat known as the carolinian forest is found. Not surprisingly, a typical example of this forest type can be found in North Carolina. In Ontario the trees found in this forest — beech, walnut and hickory — reach their northern limit along the shores of Lake Erie and western Lake Ontario. Rondeau Provincial Park is an excellent example of carolinian forest.

In colder decades there was likely too much snow for cottontails to survive here and they would have disappeared from the province or have been very rare. The opening of the land to farming and many of the crops associated with it would have vastly improved the cottontail habitat and encouraged a comeback.

Today we can see a similar occurrence with two other typical carolinian species that have recently moved into the province, the cardinal and the opossum. Although both were absent from the province 100 years ago, habitat changes and a warming trend have allowed them to extend their range into Ontario. Both appear to be here to stay.

Cottontails are true rabbits. They give birth to four to five naked and blind babies in a fur-lined nest. Hares, on the other hand, do not make nests and their young are born fully furred and able to see.

A cottontail will produce such litters three or four times a year, from February to September. If they all lived, a single pair and their offspring could, according to one estimate, produce 350,000 rabbits in five years. Most don't survive a year, as just about all of Ontario's predators eat them. Skunks and raccoons will consume very young babies. Minks, weasels, foxes, coyotes, great horned owls, hawks and many other predators will consume all ages. They are also a popular game animal with human hunters.

Many species under such pressure handle it as the cottontail does, by having the capacity to produce large numbers of offspring. This insures the survival of the species.

Not that the cottontail is totally defenceless. They run quickly for the deepest cover they can find. Their leaps may cover over ten feet and they can turn on a dime. They are also skilled at laying low. In winter they nestle down in the snow in what is known as a form. Here they are safe and virtually invisible to predators. It is only when they are discovered that they explode out and break for deeper cover. Still, the odds are against them, and sooner or later they become some predator's meal.

Look for cottontails along fence rows, in brush piles or at times in your own garden. They are very common, especially where they are protected.

Groundhog

Groundhog
Marmota monax

Weight: 4 to 12 pounds (1.5 to 4.5 kg)
Range: The entire province.

Groundhogs, or woodchucks, as they are sometimes called, belong to a branch of the squirrel family known as marmots. There are three species of marmot found in North America. The yellowbellied marmot is found along the foothills and lower slopes of the western mountains. The hoary marmot makes its home in the upper alpine meadows. Only the groundhog is found within the borders of Ontario. It is by far the least social of the three and can often be found living well away from other groundhogs. When it does choose to share a farmer's field with others of its kind, they are usually well separated and little social interaction occurs, unless of course one groundhog trespasses on another's territory, then a short chase will result.

There is an old saying that if a groundhog emerges from its den on February 2nd, Groundhog Day, and sees its shadow, then there will be six more weeks of winter. As groundhogs are hibernators that spend the winter in a deep coma-like sleep, it was thought by scientists to be highly unlikely that one would emerge from its den in the dead of winter. Groundhogs have a much lower heart rate and body temperature than does a black bear. Scientists have known for some time now that it is not unusual at all for bears to wake up and take a short stroll in mid-winter, but groundhogs were believed to be too deep into hibernation to awaken except when they were ready to feed again in the spring.

Today, thanks to much further research, scientists now know that almost all hibernating animals can and often do come out of their deep sleeps at least once during winter. So it is possible that Wiarton Willy, a well-known weather-forecasting groundhog, could emerge briefly in late February. At the very least it makes for some fun in what is often a slow news week.

A mother groundhog keeps a watchful eye on her youngsters as they play on a spring day.

In the spring it is the male who first emerges from his den. He begins by taking short walks and then seeks out emerging females with whom he will mate. This is the only time two adult woodchucks are likely to be seen together.

Young groundhogs arrive in late April or May and emerge from the den a month or so later. They are surprisingly playful, given their dour parents' lifestyles, and it is quite amusing to watch them tussle about while mother stands ever on guard.

Danger lurks everywhere, for these animals are a favourite food of great horned owls, minks, weasels and foxes. Around their own dens, however, foxes seem to tolerate groundhogs. I spent some time one Saturday watching a fox den and was surprised to see a groundhog strolling around feeding right in front of it, as if it somehow knew the resident fox had granted it immunity. Other naturalists have noted the same thing.

Groundhog dens often become homes to foxes, coyotes, skunks, snakes and a variety of other animals. The den itself may be over 5 feet deep and 30 feet long. They dig these dens by clawing at the earth with strong thick claws and kicking it out behind. Their flat noses are ideally suited for pushing the earth out too, and they use their front beaver-like teeth to cut through any roots that block their way. These teeth never stop growing and must be constantly worn down through such use.

The den itself will have a large mound around it that is hard to overlook. Here they sun themselves, rest and keep watch on the world. Other entrances, lacking this conspicuous mound, are concealed along the groundhog's feeding pathways. These are emergency entrances which I usually find after I've heard the groundhog's warning whistle and turned to see it disappear down one.

It is unusual to see one of these animals late in the fall, for they are one of the first to hibernate. I always look forward to their return in the spring and another chance to observe these interesting animals.

Groundhogs prefer open fields to den in but can be found along the edge of highways even in the far north.

Beaver

Beaver
Castor canadensis

Weight: 30 to 80 pounds (11 to 30 kg)
Range: The entire province.

Few animals have been as important to a country's development as has the beaver. It is doubtful that Canada would even exist in its present form had it not been for this overgrown rodent.

Beavers, from the 1600s until the 1830s, were popular and fashionable furbearers and very much in demand. At first this demand was met by the European beaver, but as its numbers declined due to overtrapping, the fur market looked to the newly developing Americas to supply the market.

The best fur comes from colder climates and Canada certainly has that! Beavers and other furbearers have two layers of hair or coats to insulate them against the cold. The first, the long guard hairs, are coarse and of little commercial value, but the fur undercoat is highly prized. The quest for this prize led to the creation of the Hudson's Bay Company, the exploits of the French voyageurs and the exploration of this country.

Beavers spend some time each day grooming.

The beaver paid the price for its popularity by becoming increasingly harder to find until, by the 1830s, when the demand crashed, it was a rare animal. Then, unwanted, it began a slow journey back from the edge of extinction.

Today many would argue it has been a little too successful. The problem can be best understood by looking at urban areas where rivers or streams are found. Toronto's Humber River has had beavers living within sight of the subway train for years now. Take a stroll along the bordering parkland and you'll soon discover beaver signs. They have cut down numerous trees here and even destroyed a night heron rookery.

Beavers mate for life and parent beavers will not tolerate last year's offspring sharing their part of the river. This means the young animals must seek their fortunes elsewhere. In the case of Toronto and vicinity, they have found ideal habitats in land untouched for years. As they colonized they cut down trees, much to the dismay of landowners, whose trees were consumed with great relish by these animals. I doubt that there is a pond, stream or stretch of lakeshore that has not been visited by these busy animals.

In farmland, too, they have made nuisances of themselves by building dams which flood fields or destroy woodlots. Farther north, cottagers are losing trees as well. Even in Algonquin Park they are so numerous that their impact on the environment can be seen along the entire length of Highway 60. Regulated trapping is helping control their numbers in some parts of the province without threatening the species.

It would be wrong to leave the impression that beavers are "bad." They do have a capacity to alter the landscape and this does harm some animals. It also helps some animals. Beavers create ponds in which moose and deer feed and ducks breed. Eventually these ponds become meadows where other animals come to feed too. Their dams also help control erosion and insure water levels for other species year-round.

They are also interesting animals for we humans to watch and photograph. I remember one misty morning in Algonquin when I paddled over to sit by a beaver lodge to greet the dawn. Surrounded by yellowy wisps of fog, I heard a cat-like sound coming from inside the lodge. Soon the source of this sound appeared all around me as first one, then two and then three beaver kits bobbed to the surface to play. It was a magical hour and one that anyone who is fortunate enough to find such a den can share. Just sit quietly and watch. You'll be glad you did.

Beavers have expanded their range and are now found throughout the province.

The entrance to a beaver's lodge is always below water level.

Muskrat

Muskrat
Ondatra zibethica

Weight: 1½ to 4 pounds (.5 to 1.5 kg)
Range: The entire province.

The muskrat is very much like a small beaver. It is aquatic and lives in lodges that resemble those of its larger relative.

The muskrat's lodge is not made of sticks, however. It makes its home out of cattails, and the resulting mass of vegetation can be eight feet across and three or four feet above water level. More than one family may occupy one of these homes, but most often it is used only by one.

Canada geese and other waterfowl often nest on top of the muskrat's lodge, something I've learned during the considerable time spent at a marsh near my home photographing the activity around some of these lodges. Although Canada geese choose to nest there, they don't seem overly comfortable about the presence of the mound-builders and will hiss at the muskrat when it comes near the nest.

Muskrats eat primarily marsh vegetation but will take some animal matter, such as crayfish, frogs and, I suspect, due to the goose's reaction, eggs.

Mink and weasels also visit these lodges and will eat the goose's eggs, but their main prey is the muskrat itself. Muskrats will put up a spirited defence if cornered, but flight is their best chance for survival. Many, especially the young, don't escape.

Like the rabbit, the muskrat maintains its population by having several litters a year. A single litter may contain up to 11 young, but four to seven is average. Most of the young don't survive their first year.

Muskrat habitat is wetlands and these have been disappearing throughout the province as the need for residential land has continued to grow. This is especially true for the wetlands along the Lake Ontario shorelines. All of the conservation groups in Ontario, including the Federation of Ontario Naturalists, the Ontario Federation of Anglers and Hunters, Ducks Unlimited and the Ministry of Natural Resources, see this habitat loss as one of the most pressing problems facing our wildlife. New marshes are being created to replace some of the ones being plowed under, while others are being bought up and preserved.

The marsh that I've worked for so many years is one that couldn't be saved. Over the years I've seen rails, turtles, mink, a dozen species of ducks, Canada geese, red-wing blackbirds, whitetail deer, raccoons and marsh hawks using it. When it is drained, some will simply fly on, others will suffer a more serious fate and not survive the loss of this habitat.

As for the muskrats, they will have to engage in an overland hike to the nearest river. It will be a journey fraught with danger, as cars, dogs, owls, foxes and hawks will take their toll. Those that do make it will have to contend with resident muskrats that will chase off newcomers. They will also have to learn to adapt to a new environment where there are no cattails. Homes will have to be dug into the banks like those of the river-dwelling muskrats.

Those that survive will soon recoup their losses, but the marsh that nourished them will be lost under a four-lane road. It is a small loss, really, and to its credit my city has conserved some of its marshlands for future generations. Still, for myself and the others who paused there briefly on the way to work, it will be missed.

Striped Skunk

Striped Skunk
Mephitis mephitis

Weight: 6 to 14 pounds (2 to 5 kg)
Range: The entire province.

Striped skunks are more common around cities and towns than people think they are. There is an assumption that if a skunk is about, especially at night, its telltale odour will give its presence away. That has not been my experience.

A few years ago I took one of my grade six classes on a camping trip to a local conservation area. We had eggs with us that were intended for our breakfast, and a couple of these were accidently left out when we turned in for the night.

Around midnight I heard a rustling sound just inches from my head, but I couldn't see what it was because I was inside the tent and the animal was outside. I didn't smell anything and had no thoughts of the egg thief being a skunk. A raccoon was what I expected to chase away, and you can imagine my surprise when I crawled out and encountered a skunk just a few feet away — eyeball to eyeball!

Skunks rely on their reputation as being smelly opponents and most animals don't push the issue when they see the familiar black and white pattern. As a consequence, skunks are not prone to run away. That's one reason why so many die on the roads. They apparently assume that the automobile bearing down on them will have the good sense to avoid hitting them. Having hit a couple with my car, I wish that it did have some emergency avoidance system, because a skunk's dying gift certainly stays with you for some time!

In any case, on this particular night the skunk I found myself staring at just ignored me and went about its business. I wasn't about to lose this opportunity for the sake of a few eggs, so I followed it among the children's tents as it continued its search. Not once did I smell it, nor did a single student. And I can't help wondering how many live in and around cities, quietly going about their business, keeping their smell to themselves.

On other camping trips I have woken up to a distinct "skunky" smell in the air, but almost without exception the culprit, when I was able to locate it or its tracks, was a red fox. Many animals, the fox included, have a skunk-like odour that is often more noticeable than that of the skunk itself. Indeed some animals, like dogs, will roll in the remains of a dead skunk, perhaps to disguise their own scent.

A very fat male skunk!

Few animals prey on skunks, but one night predator does, the great horned owl. They seem unperturbed by the jet of smelly oil a skunk sprays on them as it is carried off. Most animals, if hit in the face at close range, are blinded by the spray (some permanently) but not the owl. Skunks are easy prey for owls because they are fearless and do not attempt to escape, and also because they are easy to locate as they forage noisily along the forest floor in search of grubs and other insects.

Otter

Otter
Lutra canadensis

Weight: 10 to 30 pounds (4 to 11 kg)
Range: The entire province.

The weasel family is a large one that, in addition to several types of weasels, includes the marten, fisher, skunk, mink, badger and otter. Over the years I've been fortunate to have seen all of them in the wild, but the one which I have encountered most often is the river otter.

This is not surprising given the amount of time I spend around Algonquin Park's many marshes, streams and lakes looking for moose. These habitats are perfect places to see otter too, and more than once I have spent part of a day watching and photographing these playful animals.

Being predators, they are far less likely to be encountered than moose, and it is a treat to find them, for unlike other members of their family, the otter seems to enjoy play.

Personally I have never seen them tobogganing down a snowy slope on their bellies, but I don't doubt they do it. I've seen a pair of otters play tag in an icy pool, diving in and out of the remaining water, wrestling and chasing for no apparent reason other than for the fun of it.

Not that all otters are that accommodating. Usually curious, they will approach a canoeist or hiker to see what this strange creature is, but as soon as they've had a good look, they will vanish.

A few years ago a friend and I came across three otters by the Opeongo Road in Algonquin. They were on a small pond, no bigger than a few square yards and certainly very shallow. We stopped the car immediately, and they took a couple of looks at us and then dove out of sight. We felt we had them because we could see no way out of the pool except through the surrounding grass, and we figured they wouldn't do that. We never saw them again.

The following spring, near the same road, we saw what appeared to be a huge otter swimming in a small lake. We assumed that it would vanish too, but we got out and mounted our cameras on our tripods anyhow. The "huge" otter turned out to be a mating pair. The male had clamped his teeth on the female's neck and wasn't about to let go. Although we got only poor photos, we were able to watch these two animals at close range for over an hour! Even then it was we who left, not the otters.

These examples show just how unpredictable an otter can be. They can be a real bonus on a photography trip and even a quick glance is exciting.

Otters feed primarily on aquatic animals like fish and crayfish, and small mammals such as mice and muskrats. Home is usually a den in the bank, but they will take over an unused beaver lodge. The entrance in either case is always beneath the water.

Otters that are surprised to see you will woof or make sharp dog-like barks. At such times they will raise their heads upright out of the water, giving them a better view of the intruder. At other times they will chirp, growl or even whistle, depending on their mood.

It appears that this clever species is expanding its range. Once they were common along all the province's rivers and streams, but overtrapping reduced their numbers, especially in the South. In recent years there have been sightings along many of their old haunts, especially rivers just within the boundaries of cities like Toronto and Mississauga.

If you'd like to see otters, I'd suggest a slow drive along Highway 60 in Algonquin Park with frequent stops at all bodies of water. Better still, take a canoe trip back into any one of Ontario's northern parks. You just may see one of these playful animals.

Otter can be quite playful and often engage in games of tag.

In winter otters remain active as they seek prey beneath the ice and in snow covered fields.

Longtailed Weasel

Longtailed Weasel
Mustela frenata

Weight: 3 to 10 ounces (93 to 311 gm
Range: The region bordering the Great Lakes, southern Ontario, but absent from the northern half of the province.

I was sitting by a bird feeder in a conservation area one day when a sudden movement caught my eye. I looked around slowly and there was a snowy white creature staring at me. It was a longtailed weasel in its white winter coat, only its nose, eyes and tail were black. This was the first weasel I'd ever seen, and I sat very still in the hopes that it would hang around. It didn't and I saw for myself the incredible speed of this small predator as it bounded away into the forest.

The longtailed weasel is a deadly predator capable of taking rabbits several times its size. Other prey include squirrels, chipmunks, small birds, eggs, muskrats and just about anything else that is the right size and foolish enough to come too close to one of these killers.

One study has found that, should a sibling weasel be injured, the smell of its blood will cause its brothers and sisters to attack and eat it!

Apparently the ability to turn from brown to white is genetically determined. Northernmost longtailed weasels, which turn white in winter, will continue to turn white when transported south, while weasels from the South that do not turn white will not develop this ability when released into the northern range.

Weasels are a common predator, but there is no reliable place to see them. I have had some success calling them, but only after I caught a glimpse of one first. The technique is simple, all you need to do is to make a squeaking noise by sucking on your hand or fingers. This sounds like an injured mouse and the weasel will come to investigate. It won't stay long, but perhaps long enough for a clear view of this darting predator.

Weasels are well suited to hunt in the narrow openings among rocks.

Great Horned Owl

Great Horned Owl
Bubo virginianus

Length from the tip of the bill to the tail:
20 to 23 inches (51 to 58 cm)
Range: The entire province.

I still remember the first great horned owl I ever saw. A friend and fellow naturalist invited me to go "birding" with him one day at a local conservation area and he led me to a stand of hemlock trees. Here he bent down, picked up a matted grey tubular-shaped object and handed it to me. "Owl pellet," he said.

He instructed me to break it open, which I did. The grey matted material, he explained, was the hair of the owl's prey, which it "spits up" after digesting the rest of the body. Inside the mass of fur there were bones of the small animals too, and I soon held a mouse jaw between my fingers. He added that the digestive process renders the pellet perfectly harmless and safe to handle.

Then he began looking up and, sure enough, there in the upper reaches of the tree, close to the trunk, sat the owl.

I stood enthralled. Here was the Flying Tiger, the Great Stalker of the Night, the Wise Old Owl! It stared back and I was hooked. I was an owl fan, like so many others that have chanced across this bird.

I've been back several times to that stand of hemlock and I've come to appreciate just how lucky I was that first time. Seldom have I been fortunate enough to encounter another great horned owl that was willing to sit tight. Most flew away just as I approached their roosting tree.

This provided opportunities to watch something I had read about but never seen: crows mobbing an owl. Crows hate owls with a passion. Once the owl flies out of its hiding place, a crow is almost certain to spot it and out goes the distinctive call telling other crows, "Hey we got one!"

Crows have good reason to hate great horneds. Imagine a crow sitting on a nest or roosting on a limb. It is dark and the crow can't see. The owl hears or sees the crow, however, and on silent wings begins its deadly approach. The crow has little hope of escape, for even should it sense the danger, flight is a risky alternative in the pitch-black night.

Daylight affords an opportunity for them to get even and terrorize, if not kill, the owl. I've watched them dive-bomb and pester an owl for nearly an hour before the bird finally found sanctuary or the crows tired of their sport.

Great horned owls kill other animals besides crows. Raccoons, squirrels, mice, voles, rabbits, songbirds, and even skunks are fair game to this large bird of prey. They kill by driving their front two talons through the animal's skull, which results in instant death.

These owls are one of the first birds to nest. Their courting chorus of "hoos" begins in early January and by February the eggs are laid.

The eggs are laid a few days apart. This allows the owl population to control its own numbers. The first hatched will be larger than its siblings and will bully its way to the night's catch. Only if prey is abundant will the other nestlings survive. Indeed, if it is a bad year, they might well end up being part of the menu!

Great horned nests vary in location. I've photographed them on the edge of a cliff in Algonquin Park, right beside a country road in a fork of a tree, on top of a 20-foot stump, and in an old redtailed hawk's nest high above the ground. Nests tend to be re-used, but if human disturbance is too annoying the site will be deserted.

You'd think that an owl this size would avoid people. They are found in the rugged north woods, but they will also nest in city parks and local woodlots. All they need is a field or forest that provides them with enough food to live on.

A slow, careful walk in any local woodlot could well produce a view of these birds. Check the ground for owl pellets and then look up. They prefer to be near the tops of trees in places that shelter them from the eyes of crows. Once you know where to look, all it takes is time or a good guide.

Long-Eared Owl

Long-Eared Owl
Asio otus wilsonianus

Length from the tip of the bill to the tail:
13 to 16 inches (33 to 41 cm)
Range: The entire province.

Long-eared owls always have a knack of looking totally surprised when I see them. Their eyes are a bright yellow and they stare almost with a sense of bewilderment.

Little wonder, for the surprise is that I ever found them in the first place! These birds are masters of camouflage. I have stood less than 20 feet from a tree and not seen a single owl, only to take a few steps forward and have six take off in front of me. I stop, check out the tree to see if any still remain. After a few minutes of careful study I move again, certain that the tree is now devoid of owls. Naturally two more fly out.

I've played this game more times than I care to admit. You'd think by now I'd have gotten the hang of owl-spotting, but no such luck. These birds have got the art of blending in mastered. They stand as near to the trunk of their tree as they can and then stretch themselves out, elongating their bark-like markings, and presto! Instant vanishing act!

The best time to see long-eared owls is in the winter, when they arrive from the North. Look for them to roost in groups of up to 20 strong in dense vegetation bordering farmers' fields. A typical daytime roost would be in hawthorn trees growing along a stream bank. As you approach a likely area, look for the telltale "whitewash" that will coat their roosting tree. Owl droppings soon "paint" these trees, giving them a distinctive look.

Once spotted, approach slowly. You will probably see your first owl as it flies away. If you are close enough, something odd will strike you. Here is this crow-sized bird taking off and yet there is no sound! Owl feathers don't hook together like other birds' wing feathers and air passes easily through them. The result is that there is no whoosh or flutter to be heard by you or the bird's prey. It's the loudest silence I've ever heard . . . . (You'll understand that statement only after you've experienced an owl's silent departure.)

You may be lucky enough to see an owl in the summer, but for most it is a winter excursion. Long-eareds seem to be constantly changing their spots, so you will have to invest some time and effort to see them.

Long-eared owls try to make themselves look large when threatened.

Saw-Whet Owl

Saw-Whet Owl
Aegolius acadicus

Length from the tip of the bill to the tail:
  7 to 8½ inches (18 to 22 cm)
Range: All but the northern third of the province.

The saw-whet owl is one of Ontario's smallest birds of prey. It is about robin size.

Unlike great horned and long-eared owls, it lacks the tufts of feathers on its head that most people think are the owl's ears. They aren't. An owl's head consists for the most part of two huge eyes and two huge ears.

The eyes are so large, in order for the bird to see at night, that they cannot move in their sockets. That is why owls appear to be staring all the time. It also explains why they rotate their heads so much. They have to in order to see what's around them. Unlike people, they can't shift their eyes to look sideways.

It is a myth that owls see in the dark, but they can see very well by the light of stars, and a full moon is like daylight to them. Owl eyes are packed with light-sensitive cones, giving them somewhere in the neighbourhood of ten times better night vision than diurnal hunters have.

They are more than capable of locating prey in pitch darkness, not by sight but by sound. Almost as large as its eyes are an owl's ears. They are located at the sides of its head but are not perfectly aligned. One ear is slightly higher up than the other, which gives the owl two distinct readings on the source of whatever sound it hears. It is not unlike taking two compass bearings on an object and knowing that where these bearings meet is where the object is.

Lab tests with saw-whets have shown them to be so precise that they can hear the sound of a mouse from considerable distance and then, in pitch darkness, zoom in on it and take it away for a meal.

Saw-whets are reluctant to fly during the day. They choose the darkest shelter in the woodlot and there they spend the daylight hours, often with a mouse or vole to snack on. Bird-banders take advantage of their reluctance to move and simply reach up slowly and lift the bird off its perch. Once banded, the owl is gently put back, none the worse for wear.

Saw-whets migrate through southern Ontario in the early winter and early spring. It is about the only time they are relatively easy to find. It just takes a slow, careful walk through the woods. A word of caution: all owls are protected by law, so don't handle them unless licensed to do so.

Saw-whet owls are known to be excellent mousers.

Snowy Owl

Snowy Owl
Nyctea scandiaca

Length from the tip of the bill to the tail:
 20 to 26 inches (51 to 66 cm)
Range: The tundra regions at the extreme north of Ontario for most of the year, but many move into southern Ontario in the winter months.

Many people are surprised to learn that every winter snowy owls are regular visitors to southern Ontario. These owls are usually thought of as being year-round residents of the Arctic and for some that is no doubt true.

The snowy owl is an Arctic bird. Its white colour and feathered feet attest to that, and in good years it can survive quite nicely the long winter and bitter cold of the North. A "good year," however, is determined by the availability of its main food source, the lemming. If lemmings are abundant, then the snowy owls will produce more young. In winter some of these young birds will be forced to migrate south because lemmings are by then scarce and there are more predators competing for them. By the same token, a bad lemming crop will result in fewer surviving owls, and those that do may have to head south as well in order to survive. Either way, there are usually snowy owls wintering in southern Ontario.

One reason they tend to stop here rather than in the northern forests is that southern Ontario farmland bears a strong resemblance to the tundra. Both are flat, generally open expanses of land ideally suited to the snowy's hunting style.

There is also an abundance of food. Snowy owls take voles, mice and other small animals that are found around these open fields. They usually perch on some high object, a fence post, small hill, tree or even a lamppost, to watch for some movement. Unlike other owls, they hunt as much during the day as they do at night.

The various spits and new parklands in the Toronto region are good places to look for these owls. Here they prey on ducks and even gulls.

Only on rare occasions have I had an animal seek me out to help it survive and the most dramatic of these involved a gull and a snowy owl.

A naturalist friend and I had heard that there was a snowy owl by the mouth of the Humber River, so we went down one evening to see if we could get any pictures. It was cold and crisp and we had no luck. The sun had set and we were about to pack it in when the cries of a gull caught our attention. We soon spotted the gull zigzagging madly against the darkening sky. Then we saw the cause of this odd behaviour. An owl was attacking it!

In its panic the gull took refuge on the ground where, for some reason, the owl couldn't make the kill. The owl would appear to fly off and the gull would take to the air. Immediately the owl would return and hit it with its talons. About then the gull spotted us and landed right at our feet, almost begging us to protect it. The snowy circled a few times and vanished into the night, leaving the three of us breathless.

Unfortunately the cold was creeping in under our winter parkas and we had to leave. The gull was still huddled on the ground as we pulled away, but I have no doubt about what happened later that night.

Besides the Toronto region another good spot to look for snowy owls is on Amherst Island, just east of Kingston. Great grey owls and a variety of hawks may also be seen. You might also try farmers' fields and local airports. If you see one that has distinct black markings on it, it is a female; males are almost pure white.

Osprey

Osprey
Pandion haliaetus carolinenius

Length from the tip of the bill to the tail:
21 to 24 inches (53 to 61 cm)
Wing span: 4½ to 6 feet (137 to 183 cm)
Range: The entire province.

When I was a kid going to cottages and camping in the 1950s and 60s, I never saw an osprey. The reason was simple: there weren't many around to see. They were victims of the now infamous DDT chemical spraying of that era. This spray was used to kill off insect pests, which it did very well, at first. The problem was that other animals, including songbirds, ate the poisoned insects and in turn became poisoned too.

Scientists studying this deadly food chain noted that the higher up they traced the chemical, the more long-lasting its effects. The osprey, thanks to its role as a large predator, sat near the top of these food chains and it suffered accordingly. They didn't die, for the DDT wasn't powerful enough to kill them outright, but it did cause them to lay eggs with very brittle shells that cracked easily.

Virtually no young ospreys survived to carry on the next generations. It looked like the species would vanish not only from Ontario but from the continent.

I saw my first osprey in 1970. My dad and my fiancée were out fishing with me in Algonquin Park when we heard a loud splash. At first we thought it was a large fish jumping, but when we looked we were astonished to see a large black and white bird emerging, with much splashing, from the water.

Since then I've been a fan of ospreys, or fish hawks, as they are also called. I've photographed them in Florida, Yellowstone, Jasper and Banff, but I am proud to say my best shots have come from Ontario. Thanks to the banning of DDT in 1972, the species has been making a steady comeback throughout its range and especially here in this province.

All it needs is some protection (it is fully protected under International Treaty with the United States), shallow lakes with abundant fish and a place to nest. These needs are met in many spots throughout the province, including Luther Marsh (near Orangeville) and stretches along the Lake Superior shoreline, but nowhere are they better met than in Lindsay District.

Lindsay District and the region surrounding it encompasses several large, shallow lakes known as the Kawarthas. These lakes, thanks to the limestone rock

A young osprey is watched carefully by one of its parents.

Osprey have made a comeback in Ontario since being nearly wiped out by the chemical spraying of DDT.

underlying them, have not suffered from acid rain and are rich in fish. Some of the province's best muskie, bass and walleye fishing can be had here.

These fish are also fair game for the osprey, but so are the large variety of non-game fish that abound here. In terms of food, it is an ideal location for these large birds of prey.

Nesting sites are a problem. There are few large trees left in the region, and at first the osprey had to make do with these. Soon though the expanding population was forced to nest wherever it could, including stumps in the marshes, just inches above water level, or telephone poles. The Ministry of Natural Resources, Ontario Hydro and local conservation groups embarked on a program of replacing unsuitable nesting sites with four-legged platforms called quadropods. The plan worked and today well over 60 of these artificial nest sites are occupied and producing osprey.

Fishermen and -women have welcomed the birds, for the most part, although a few complaints about ospreys spoiling the fishing do surface from time to time. Generally, though, the birds offer an entertaining show as they plunge feet-first into the water after their prey.

Ospreys don't linger in the water. They take off with rapid strokes of their wings, lifting their prey after them. Sometimes the prey is too heavy, leaving the osprey little choice but to swim to shore with it or drown. Letting go is not something they do readily. Once airborne they carry the fish in as streamlined a manner as possible, with the head aligned under their bodies.

I once saw an osprey do a remarkable thing, something I have never heard of one doing before. The bird, a male I think, repeatedly flew just inches above the water, unzipping the lake with its prey, a small fish, and I can only conclude it was washing it. It then fed on the fish before bringing it to the nest, where the female fed the rest to her hungry brood.

The young ospreys will winter along the Gulf of Mexico for two or three years before returning to the area where they hatched. They will likely encounter their parents when they return, because the birds use the same nesting site year after year. The nesting pair will not tolerate other ospreys near them, and so the youngsters will fly off in search of new territory in which to start their families. They may even show up on a lake near you. If they do, welcome them.

An osprey lands on a hydro pole with its catch.

Ontario's Eagles

Bald Eagle
Haliacetus leucocephalus
Golden Eagle
Aquila chrysaetos

Length from the tip of the bill to the tail:
  30 to 40 inches (76 to 102 cm)
Range: All but the northern third of the province.
Wing Span: 6 to 7½ feet (183 to 229 cm)
Range: Spotty throughout the province.

Ontario is home to both golden and bald eagles, although the numbers of the former are quite low. There are almost certainly less than 10 golden eagle nesting sites in the entire province and most of those are in the Hudson Bay lowlands.

Bald eagles are more numerous, especially in the Lake of the Woods area in northwestern Ontario. In the south they are rare, although in the 1800s it is said that there wasn't a mile stretch of Lake Erie or Lake Ontario shoreline that didn't have a pair of these birds of prey. Today there are perhaps seven nests in all of southern Ontario. What happened?

DDT cannot be blamed for the disappearance of the bald eagle. Their downfall in the 1800s and early part of this century was due to the same thing that threatens wildlife species today: habitat destruction.

Eagles need tall trees to build their massive nests in, and these trees were quickly cleared by farmers and loggers. They also need fish to feed on, but the mills on

Only three golden eagle nests are known in Ontario.

many of the rivers clogged the streams and caused the native fish stocks to dwindle.

Eagles also need privacy. Ospreys can be very tolerant of people, but eagles aren't. Besides, the presence of these large birds made some folks uncomfortable, fearing the loss of sheep, calves or even children, so they shot the eagles.

Bald eagles, for all their size, are not inclined to take large prey. They will scavenge dead animals when they can, but they prefer fish and waterfowl. Golden eagles do prey on small mammals and probably could take a lamb or a stray cat, but such losses would be offset by the good they do in controlling crop-destroying rodents. Of course here in Ontario there are so few of these birds that they are almost never seen by people in any case.

The Canadian Wildlife Service's land on Long Point (Lake Erie) is the site of an ongoing effort to restore bald eagles to their former range in the southern part of the province. Eaglets have been trapped from areas of healthy eagle numbers and released on Long Point to build up the local wild population. Unfortunately the area is closed off to all visitors and viewing opportunities are nil.

Rondeau Provincial Park has active eagle nests, and both adult and young birds are seen regularly around Rondeau Bay. It is probably the best area in the province south of the Lake of the Woods to see them. They can also be seen when they migrate through the province on their way south to Chesapeake Bay and the Mississippi wintering grounds (see the section on the redtailed hawk for details).

Redtailed Hawk

Redtailed Hawk
Buteo jamaicensis

Length from the tip of the bill to the tail:
19 to 25 inches (48 to 63.5 cm)
Range: All but the most northern portion of the province.

The shrill screeching call of a redtailed hawk as it soars overhead is a familiar sound to hikers in southern Ontario. These large hawks are the most noticeable of Ontario's hawks because they often nest close to places frequented by people. To see them you should look for their nests in the tallest tree in the woodlot.

It is not uncommon to see several of these birds or their nests on any country drive throughout the rural parts of the province.

Another reason for their high visibility is that they hunt during daylight hours, unlike the nighttime predators, the owls.

There are three families of hawks found in Ontario. They are the buteos, the falcons and the accipters. The redtailed hawk is a typical buteo. It has long, broad wings, ideal for soaring on the

Redtailed hawks are the species most often seen during country drives in Ontario.

updrafts of heated air from farmers' fields, and a short, broad tail. Other Ontario buteos include the broadwinged hawk and the rough-legged hawk.

The tiny sparrow hawk, or kestrel, as it is more properly known, is the most common falcon to be found in the province. It is the small hawk seen most often "helicoptering" in place over a field, waiting for a mouse to show itself. Like other falcons, it has long, pointed wings and a slender body.

The fastest flyer in the world, the peregrine falcon, is a larger version of the kestrel. It is making a comeback in the province after almost vanishing thanks to DDT poisoning.

The accipters are rarely seen because, unlike the other families which hunt in open areas, these hawks hunt the forests. Their bodies are compromises, halfway between buteo and falcon in shape. Their wings are short to allow them to fly easily between branches and yet, like buteos, they are broad enough to permit limited soaring. Their tails are long and falcon-like, permitting them to change direction rapidly as they follow their prey's flight for safety. The goshawk is typical of these birds but is rarely seen.

Virtually all of Ontario's hawks, eagles and osprey can be seen during their migration in the fall at one of two ideal sites. Hawk Cliff, on Lake Erie near Port Stanley, is located south of London. Between August and December nearly 20,000 hawks pass over this spot on their way south. The other spot is Ball's Falls Conservation Area near Grimsby. Bald eagles and peregrine falcons are seen here on rare occasions. The best viewing at Ball's Falls is in September.

Winter offers some excellent viewing, as many Arctic hawks, such as the rough-legged, move south and frequent Ontario's open fields. Airports are an ideal spot to see them.

Once spring arrives, the redtailed again regains its position as the most visible hawk in the province.

Kestrels are small falcons often seen hovering above fields.

The peregrine falcon is the subject of intensive efforts by conservationists to restore it to its former range.

Redtailed hawks prefer to nest in the tallest tree they can find.

Tundra Swan

Tundra Swan
Olor columbianus

Length from the tip of the bill to the tail:
 48 to 55 inches (122 to 140 cm)
Range: Stops over in the province on its way to and from its Arctic breeding sites. A very few pair nest along the shore of Hudson Bay.

The tundra swan has made a comeback in numbers since hitting rock bottom around the early 1950s. Today there are some 93,000 of these birds wintering along the Atlantic seaboard, especially in the Chesapeake Bay area. A large number of these swans stop in Ontario on their way north to their tundra nesting sites.

There was a time when these swans nested within Ontario's borders. All of these nesting birds confined their breeding grounds to the shoreline of Hudson Bay and they quickly disappeared with the advent of the fur-trapping empires along that shore. The birds were shot to provide food by both natives and whites.

It has only been in the last few years that they have again returned to nest there, and there are hopes that they will soon establish a larger presence.

Another swan, the trumpeter swan, also nested in this province. There are records of it nesting in marshes in southern Ontario from the 1600s, but it too disappeared as guns were introduced.

In a bold undertaking, the Ministry of Natural Resources is attempting to re-introduce this native species by importing trumpeter swan eggs from nest sites in the West and placing them in mute swan nests on the Lake Ontario shoreline.

The mute swan is a European species brought over at the beginning of this century to decorate parks and gardens. Many escaped and established wild breeding pairs along the Great Lakes. While beautiful to look at, they are very aggressive birds and have harmed local waterfowl by chasing them out of ponds. The Ministry hopes that by replacing mute swan eggs with the trumpeter's eggs they can control the former's number while re-establishing a native species. So far they have met with only limited success. However, both species can frequently

Each March, thousands of tundra swans gather at Alymer's Police College where they may be viewed.

be seen along the Toronto lakefront.

For truly spectacular swan viewing, March is the month. Just north of Aylmer, the Ontario Police College has set aside a portion of its land as a migrating swan stopover. Feed is provided and it is possible to see from the viewing stand over 3,000 of these birds as they come and go.

Further south on the Lake Erie shoreline are three parks that provide swan viewing as well. Rondeau Provincial Park and Point Pelee National Park offer good views, but Long Point Provincial Park and the adjoining causeway offers the best. I like to arrive around two in the afternoon, just as the birds start to raft up in the bays before flying inland to feed. From then until sunset you are likely to see the swans moving about in flocks of between 3 and 20 birds. The noisy squadrons sometimes come out just over your head, providing great views of these birds.

Some 5,000 of them will be there. However, if the ice has not gone out, they may be hard to see except at dusk, when they come in to feed. Sometimes they can be seen in the nearby fields, although you will have to ask around to find out where these may be. I find this type of viewing more exciting than the Aylmer site, but it can also be much more frustrating — there have been days when I couldn't find the birds.

The swans in March do provide one of the best wildlife viewing opportunities in the province and are well worth the time. I highly recommend this late-winter jaunt.

Mute swans are an introduced species of swan from Europe.

*Efforts to restore the Trumpeter swan may one day
see this species again nesting in Ontario.*

Mallard Duck

Mallard Duck
Anas platyrhynchos

Length from the tip of the bill to the tail:
18 to 27 inches (46 to 69 cm)
Range: The entire province.

Mallard ducks can be easily seen in just about any city park in the province. They appear so tame that it is hard to believe they can be smart and wary when they are hunted. Yet most hunters will tell you that they are not at all an easy bird to bag.

Mallards are puddle ducks or dabblers. These types of ducks are typically found in shallow marshes and rivers rather than on large lakes and bays in the province. They feed by dabbling, turning bottoms up as they feed on the floor of the wetland. They can dive but seldom do so.

Puddle ducks are the ones seen in farmers' fields too. These ducks take off straight into the air from the water, unlike diving ducks. Typical puddle ducks found in the province include the black duck, pintail, widgeon, gadwall, blue-wing teal and shoveller duck.

Black ducks are closely related to mallards.

The most common of these is the mallard. The most spectacular is the wood duck. Unlike the other puddle ducks, which nest on the ground, the wood duck chooses to nest in trees. The male is the more brightly coloured sex in almost all species of duck, but none more so than the drake woody.

Ducks, as a rule, mate for life. The female insists on being courted in late winter despite her lifelong pairing. The male mallard will dutifully perform his bobbing dance for her as early as February. As the season progresses he will have to battle other males for her affection, and some of these fights can be quite violent by duck standards. A trip to the local waterfront or duck pond to watch these squabbles is always worthwhile. Somehow it all gets sorted out by April.

Once the eggs are laid the male leaves the hen and begins to enter the eclipse phase. This is the time of year when he moults and is flightless. I have read that male mallards totally desert their mates during this time of year, but my own observations tend to suggest that the pairs stay closer together than was originally believed.

The young ducklings can swim immediately after hatching and must get their own food. They will imprint on the first moving object they see, which if all goes well will be their mother. Once imprinted they will follow the object of their affection until the imprinting wears off in mid to late summer. There are many reports of them imprinting on human foster parents and even some that imprinted on dogs!

Ducklings, like all young, are both the future of the species and its surplus. Many are taken by raccoons, mink and large fish, others fall to hunters' guns, but a few survive to carry on their species. Mallard numbers are on the increase across all of Canada.

Mallard ducks fly at about 60 kilometers (40 miles) per hour.

Wood ducks nest in trees.

Common Goldeneye

Common Goldeneye
Bucephala clangula

*Length from the tip of the bill to the tail: 16 to 20 inches
(41 to 51 cm)
Range: The entire province.*

The common goldeneye is a typical diving duck. The "divers" are ducks that are quite adept at swimming underwater after their food. Other members of this group found in Ontario include the bufflehead, oldsquaw, canvasback, redhead, the three species of mergansers, scaup and ring-necked duck.

All of these species show a marked preference for large lakes and bays. Rafts of scaup and oldsquaw ducks can easily be seen on most of the Great Lakes during winter. Smaller numbers of the other divers are often mixed in with them too.

Divers must run along the surface of the water before taking off, a behaviour which makes it easy to distinguish them from puddle ducks. Another distinctive feature is the placement of their legs. Puddle ducks have their legs placed more or less in the centre of their bodies, while divers have theirs located to the rear, giving them an awkward loon-like appearance.

Most people assume that all ducks quack. Some, like the mallard, do, but there are a number of species that whistle or peep. Male goldeneyes, while usually quiet, make a rasping "speer speer" call when courting females in the late winter and early spring.

They are nicknamed the "whistlers" not because of their calls but because of the whistling sound their wings make while in flight.

Many diving ducks nest on the northern tundra, but not the common goldeneye. The female makes a down-filled nest as high up in a tree as she can. This provides for a measure of protection against predators, but it also poses a problem when the ducklings hatch. Like all ducks, they can feed themselves almost immediately after hatching. They can walk, hop and peep, but they can't fly. The problem is that there is not a whole lot of food available around the nest site, which may be 60 feet above the ground.

The solution? Jump!

Urged on by their mother, these tiny babies begin (and sometimes end) their lives by leaping out of the nest. Their downy feathers provide some protection to cushion the landing and most survive. Then comes the walk to the water. Guided by the hen, they must avoid foxes, owls and other predators. Once on the marsh, they must then contend with bass and muskies.

There are always a few common goldeneye along the Toronto waterfront and I make frequent excursions there during the winter to watch them. One year I was treated to a rare sight. A snowy owl had also arrived from the North and had taken up winter quarters in the same area I was working in. I watched this owl hunt the goldeneye and oldsquaw with interest. It would fly low across the lake, scattering ducks ahead of it. Some would run on the water before diving, while others just crash-dived. The owl would then circle and with deadly precision pick up a duck when it bobbed to the surface.

It was a fascinating display of predators and prey in action played out against the backdrop of Toronto's skyline.

The common goldeneye is also a tree nesting duck.

These oldsquaw ducks commonly winter on the Great Lakes.

Buffleheads are one of the smallest ducks in Ontario.

The hooded merganser is another tree nesting duck of Ontario's north.

The shoveller duck has a bill that looks much like a shovel.

Canada Goose

Canada Goose
Branta canadensis

Length from the tip of the bill to the tail:
  23 to 45 inches (58 to 114 cm)
Range: The entire province.

Many waterfowl do not fly in "V" formation, but the Canada goose does. Their wavering V's are a familiar sight across the province as they head south in winter and north in spring.

Ontario is home to many subspecies, including the Hudson Bay Canada goose and the greater Canada goose. To most of us, the two subspecies are impossible to tell apart unless they are standing side by side (the greaters are larger). Generally speaking, the ones found wintering around the lakes belong to the latter group. These are all descended from a few pairs kept in captivity at the Niska Waterfowl Research Centre in Guelph, Ontario.

The centre worked hard in the 1950s to save this subspecies of Canada geese from becoming extinct. As its mated pairs produced offspring, local conservation and hunting groups released them into the wild in the hopes they would survive. Many did and their offspring were shipped to places in the United States where the subspecies had also disappeared or was about to.

The nightly arrival of thousands of Canada geese at Jack Miner's Sanctuary in Kingsville is well worth the trip.

Today over 50,000 giant Canadas can be found year-round between Hamilton and Oshawa. They are suffering from somewhat of a population explosion and suitable housing is at a premium. As a result, these birds have taken to nesting just about anywhere there is water. Ponds on golf courses, farms and parks, no matter how small, will have a resident pair of geese. Many of these nests are vulnerable to predators and entire broods are often lost.

There are prime nesting sites too and these are occupied by the most aggressive birds. Males are quick to chase off other males that enter their territory. Females will also join in the battle if another pair encroaches on the nest site. Dominance shifts as each pair chases or retreats to and from their own territory, until a sort of "no goose-land" is agreed upon.

Goslings don't seem to be too concerned about such matters. It is not uncommon to see a pair of adults swim by with two young in tow and then return with eight only a few moments later. Goslings, it seems, are unable to tell one Canada goose from another and will follow any adult bird.

The coming of fall means that most geese will migrate. Flight after flight will go overhead as the geese that nested on the tundra head south. Geese along the Lake Ontario shore will winter there, relying on the ample daily feedings provided by scores of birdlovers.

There is one remarkable spot to see wild Canada geese and that is Jack Miner's Sanctuary in Kingsville. Here, at peak times in the spring and fall, it is possible to see 10,000 geese as they fly in from Lake Erie to feed on the corncobs put out for them. To insure a good show and to give visitors a chance to appreciate the birds in their full glory, the geese are put up each afternoon by the sanctuary.

The show achieves its goal, but for something truly awe-inspiring, stay for the sunset flight. To see thousands of these birds coming in against an orange or pink sky is a sight that will stay with you a lifetime!

Common Loon

Common Loon
Gavia immer

Size: 28 to 36 inches (71 to 91 cm) (goose size)
Range: All of Ontario.
Description: Breeding plumage (pictured)
Winter plumage: grey and white

The long, mournful cry of a loon heard above a crackling fire just before turning in is perhaps one of Ontario's most cherished sounds. It certainly is one of mine.

Loons and Ontario's North are linked in most cottagers' and campers' minds. Spend any time among the lakes and pines of the Canadian Shield and you'll come away enchanted by the haunting cries and amused by the birds' maniacal laughter.

Surprisingly it is a sound that can also be heard along the shores of the Great Lakes in the spring and fall. The birds pause here during their migration to and from their southern wintering grounds to feed on the lakes' abundant fish. Their songs come as a pleasant surprise to strollers whose thoughts are not at all on cottage country. I've heard loons at Long Point on Lake Erie as early as late March and regularly hear them in late fall on my photography trips to the Toronto lakeshore.

The loons won't breed there, however. They need the protection of the North's smaller, more sheltered lakes. These birds are very poor walkers and travel only a few feet from the shore in order to nest. The nest site must be nearly at water level for the birds to find it suitable, and this poses a problem on big lakes.

Rough water, due either to winds or powerboat wakes, threatens these nesting sites and explains why the birds seldom nest on big lakes. Cottagers who spend time on lakes where boating is common will likely see loons in increasing numbers towards the end of the summer, as the birds fly onto these lakes for fish. The young stay on the more sheltered water until they are able to join their parents.

Loons call to communicate with their mates and to warn other loons to stay away from the pair's territory. Sometimes a lake will have more than one pair on it, and when the four birds start to sing, the resulting lyrical duel can add greatly to an evening around the campfire as the calls echo off the surrounding hills.

Loons feed on small fish, for the most part, but will also eat crayfish, frogs and aquatic insects. To get their prey they can dive to depths over 200 feet and stay under for well over a minute. This habit earned them their European name of Northern Diver.

When their two eggs hatch, the parents will almost immediately take the youngsters into the water. When the small loons tire of swimming, they climb onto a parent's back. This works fine until the parent dives. The chicks, unable to dive, are quite capable swimmers and just bob along on the surface until their parent returns with dinner.

I've seen loons on one lake with newborn young and on the next lake encountered grown chicks that were almost equal in size to the adults. Apparently the timing of loon hatching varies from one pair to another.

I've also seen up to 15 loons together in late August. All the birds were adults (the young are grey and white) and seemed to be unconcerned with territory or mates. I imagine that on surrounding smaller lakes the young birds were waiting patiently for the return of their parents. I suspect, too, that such a gathering marks the end of the summer season and the beginning of the migration. Such gatherings of loons are most likely due to a concentration of prey fish.

Whatever the reason, they herald the imminent departure of the birds and, soon after, the cottagers. By mid-October the lakes will be quiet and those, like myself, that linger on will miss the yodels, moans and laughter of the loon.

Great Blue Heron

Great Blue Heron
Ardea herodias

Length from the tip of the bill to the tail:
42 to 52 inches (107 to 132 cm)
Range: Southern two thirds of the province. Absent from the northern region.

Most who see this long-necked bird will incorrectly identify it as a crane. There are few if any cranes living wild in Ontario (although there are many sandhill cranes found in the West), but blue herons are common.

Herons fly with their long necks held in an "S" curve, while cranes fly with theirs outstretched.

Ontario is home to several members of the heron family. Little green herons can be found hunting small crayfish and minnows on many streams. Black-crowned night herons, bitterns and American egrets are also sighted at marshes, particularly along Lake Erie.

As a rule, the further south you are in this province the more species of birds you are likely to encounter. Places like Point Pelee and Rondeau Provincial Park are excellent spots for serious birders. American egrets are common sights here, for example, but are almost never seen around Lake Ontario's marshes.

The great blue heron is the largest of its family found in North America. It is a wading bird and can be found in marshes, swamps and lakes throughout most of the province. To watch one of these birds stalk its prey is to watch a master hunter at work. They move very slowly, one leg at a time, and then pause. The neck is stretched out so that the heron has a vantage point well away from any disturbance its feet might cause. When prey is sighted, the neck is withdrawn to its characteristic "S" shape and then suddenly the bill is thrust forward, spearing the victim.

The green heron is sometimes called the up-the-creek-bird due to its habit of moving upstream to fish.

Food consists of frogs, crayfish, snakes, minnows, and other fish, all of which the heron swallows whole. As soon as it finishes one meal, it is ready to hunt again, unless there are young to feed.

Herons nest in trees in colonies and it is an amazing sight to see these large birds landing delicately on the uppermost limbs of tall trees. Their nests are huge and that, combined with the large amount of droppings they deposit, can have very detrimental effects on the trees used by the colony.

The size of heron rookeries vary. Some have only a few nests, while others might have up to 40 nests or more. As a rule, the larger rookeries are in the South, while ones on the Canadian Shield have fewer birds.

Many of these colonies are located in farmers' woodlots, others are found in swamps. It is surprising how many such colonies exist in the southern portion of the province, but most are on private land. One, located at the Luther Marsh Wildlife Management Area west of Orangeville, is visible from the shore and by canoe. It is, however, closed to the public during breeding season. Even so, it is well worth the effort of paddling along the marsh to see these nesting sites, even after most of the birds are long gone in August. An added bonus of the canoe ride is the strong chance of seeing ospreys, ducks, geese and even other types of herons.

In fall the marsh is open to duck hunters, so a visit at this time may or may not be of interest.

In the spring breeding herons sport a long black feather trailing behind their ears. Juveniles and nonbreeding adults lack this feather in the fall.

Should you be fortunate enough to see one of these birds, take a few minutes and watch it. If you are like me, the bird will transport your imagination back to the days of dinosaurs and pteradons.

Canada Jay

Canada Jay
Perisoreus canadensis

Length from the tip of the bill to the tail:
 10 to 13 inches (25 to 33 cm)
Range: All of the province except the southern farming regions.

The Canada jay has a variety of names, but two of the most popular are "whisky-jack" and "grey jay." All three names are appropriate. The Canada jay is found for the most part in Canada. Where it does wander into the United States, it is associated with typical Canadian-type pine forests.

Its call is said by many to sound like its other name, "whisky-jack," and it is a grey colour.

It is also a member of the jay family, which includes the crow, raven and bluejay. This family is reputed to be one of the most intelligent among birds.

By the time you head north in May to open a cottage or go fishing, this bird will have already nested and reared its young. It is, along with the great horned owl, one of the earliest nesting birds in the province.

A visit to Algonquin Park in winter may not produce a single moose, otter or fox, but will almost certainly lead you to a Canada jay. These birds are known for their tameness and their bold attacks on bacon, bread or anything else a camper might leave out during the summer — but this doesn't hold a candle to their winter antics.

Place some seeds, bread or even bits of meat in your hand and sooner or later one of these birds will glide in to perch. They won't stay long, but no worry, another one usually shows up to take its place.

They are fond of pine seeds which, along with buds, they glue together using saliva and save for times when food is scarce.

I enjoy their company whenever they are about and always look forward to our next meeting, even though they can be bold guests. A visit to the Canadian Shield just wouldn't be the same without seeing some of these "friendly" birds.

Canada jays are among the first birds to nest in Ontario.

Bird Feeders

In this book I have tried to give the reader some ideas about how and where wildlife might be seen. I've suggested places near and far, but it can be very rewarding to spend some time in your own backyard. Almost anyone, from an apartment dweller to the owner of a country estate, can attract wildlife, especially birds, to their window. All you need to do is put out some feed.

True, you might just get common everyday city birds such as the pigeon or the house sparrow, but even these can give you an understanding of bird behaviour. You might even find them special in their own right.

I must confess that when I set up a feeder I am hoping more for native birds than those introduced by the European settlers to make them feel at home.

Begin feeding in November, preferably before the first snowfall. The reason for this is that the birds must come to know that food is available or they will migrate south (or to your neighbour's feeder). You will have more success, too, if there is plenty of shelter for the birds to roost in while they feed.

By the dead of winter you could have a real show going on as one species after another visits. The more variety of food and suet you supply, the more types of birds you get. You will also notice that they each have particular patterns of coming and going. After years of photographing at such feeders, here is my observation of that order.

First come the smaller birds, the black-capped chickadees, redpolls and tree sparrows. They must come in more often in order to maintain their high metabolisms.

Next come the medium-size birds. Nuthatches, the only bird that can go up or down a tree face first, will visit briefly and fly off. Bluejays are wary but will usually come in before cardinals. Grosbeaks, if they are around, will come in often and boldly.

Woodpeckers, either downy (the smaller) or hairy, come and go all the time. They are especially fond of suet. The males have a red band on the back of their heads, the females don't.

The last to come in are the mourning doves. They are larger and don't need to eat as often, and they are about the most wary of all the birds.

If you are lucky you may get small hawks (kestrels) or owls (screech and saw-whet) hanging around, taking the odd songbird for dinner. That may upset some, but for me the predator and the prey are equal in value and interest. I enjoy watching the two go about their lives — and to do it from my kitchen, that's an added bonus!

The sex of a downy woodpecker can be determined by the colour of the back of its head. Males have a red streak.

Blackcapped chickadees are usually the first bird in to a feeder in winter.

Whitebreasted nuthatches can go up or down a tree trunk head first.

Although plainer than the male, the female Cardinal is still a beautiful bird.

Tree sparrows come down from the arctic to winter in Ontario.

Mourning doves are among the most cautious of Ontario's song birds.

*Bluejays have a variety of calls but the one most
often heard sounds like "thief! thief!".*

Massassauga Rattler

Massassauga Rattler
Sistrurus catenatus

Length: to 30 inches (76 cm)
Range: Confined to the Georgian Bay and Lake Huron shoreline.

The massassauga rattlesnake is on Canada's endangered species list and is therefore protected against harm. It may seem odd to afford protection to a potentially dangerous species, but in point of fact it makes good sense.

First, the danger from rattlesnakes is not as acute as western novels would have you believe. Having tramped around rattlesnake country for a good many years now, I have never seen one unless I set out to look for one in the first place. I have interviewed park naturalists in Georgian Bay National Park, people whose jobs take them through an area with perhaps the densest population of massassaugas in the province, and few have ever seen a wild one. The point is that these snakes avoid human beings.

Even on those rare encounters when the two meet, the snake goes out of its way to warn off its "enemy" by noisily rattling its tail. Nor can they strike that far. Contrary to a popular belief, they do not leap through the air but can only strike at objects that are fairly close (about one third their body length).

Their bites are painful and will cause humans to become very sick, but they are seldom fatal to adults. Children, due to smaller body mass, are more likely to die from bites because the poison isn't diluted as much in their bloodstreams.

On the positive side, these snakes help control rodent numbers and can be beneficial. I suppose, however, that the main reason to afford them protection is that they are another species sharing this planet and have a right to live.

A side benefit is the indirect aid massassauga protection provides other snakes. Several other species resemble this snake and have in the past been killed because of this resemblance. One species, the eastern hognose snake (*Heterodon platyrhinos*) is endangered because of its resemblance to rattlesnakes. Actually it is a delightful snake that can really put on a good show. It will hiss and flare its neck, looking for all the world like a cobra, and then when that doesn't work it will roll over and play dead. It is nonpoisonous and, except for its bluff, totally placid. Unfortunately it likes beaches. Swimmers are generally unnerved by its behaviour, and it is often killed by protective parents.

Another water-loving snake is the water snake (*Nerodia sipedon*). These are big snakes by Ontario standards (up to 53 inches/135 cm) and are often mistaken for water moccasins, a snake not found in this province. They are aggressive and will bite, but they are not deadly, and I had one as a classroom pet for several months that was truly well behaved.

Ontario is home to many snakes, all of which are interesting reptiles in their own right. Should you wish to see them, start turning over rocks and looking under old logs and you will soon encounter them. A word of warning, however: Turn the rocks over very carefully along the Georgian Bay shore.

The massassauga rattlesnake is found along the shores of Georgian Bay, Lake Huron and Lake Erie.

The milk snake is a harmless snake that is often mistaken for a "rattler".

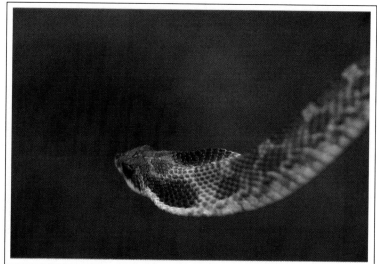

*Despite its cobra-like appearance
the Eastern hognose snake
is not dangerous.*

*Hognose snakes prefer sandy areas. Unfortunately so do people and this has
caused a rapid decline in the numbers of these peaceful snakes.*

The green snake is seldom seen but can be found in southern Ontario fields.

The common garter snake is the snake most often seen by people in the Province.

Watersnakes are large and are often encountered by people out fishing.

Blanding's Turtle

Blanding's Turtle
Emydoidea blandingi

Length: to 9 inches (23 cm)
Range: Lakes, rivers and streams of southern Ontario.

Blanding's turtle can easily be identified by its bright yellow throat. It is listed as rare in Ontario, although in some parts of its range it is very common.

I've encountered them on canoe trips down the Humber River in Toronto and at Rattray Marsh in Mississauga. They are fairly common in the marshes at the tip of Rondeau Provincial Park on Lake Erie too.

Turtles are reptiles and exhibit all of that class's characteristics. They are coldblooded and so must control their body temperature by moving in and out of sunlight as the summer days progress. That is why they are often found sunning themselves on logs. What they are in fact doing is warming up their blood, for unlike warmblooded animals their blood takes on the temperature of its sur-roundings. They must guard against becoming too hot as well as too cold. Turtles that stay out in the sun can actually boil their brains, causing them to become addled. Death is the result. To avoid this they will return to water to cool down again, constantly regulating their temperature.

Being reptiles, turtles must lay their eggs on dry land. Snapping turtles generally do this late in the spring, while the smaller turtles nest in early summer. Turtle eggs are much favoured by raccoons and foxes and are often dug up shortly after they are laid.

How do turtles survive Ontario's winter if they are coldblooded? They dig deep beneath the mud at the bottom of their pond or lake and there they hibernate. So long as the water above them does not freeze completely through, they will survive. If the mud surrounding them should freeze, then they die, and in shallower ponds this does happen.

The best time to look for turtles is in the spring, when they are most likely to be sunning themselves. You will find them on virtually every body of water in southern Ontario.

Blanding's turtle can be easily identified by its bright yellow throat patch.

Snapping Turtle

Snapping Turtle
Chelydra serpentina

Length: to 18 inches (46 cm)
Weight: to 70 pounds (26 kg)
Range: Southern third of the province.

When I was young and foolish I snorkelled along after a fairly large snapping turtle, watching her feed on some bass a fisherman had left in the water to keep fresh. I don't suppose I was in any real danger, but as I watched those powerful jaws clamp on the fish's body my imagination ran rampant. I could picture one of those turtles emerging from the depths below to clamp onto my foot and drag me down with it. Of course that is nonsense and I have since found the snapping turtle to be an added bonus on my trips around the province to photograph other wildlife.

I don't often see them, for unlike other turtles they are much less likely to be seen sunning themselves, preferring to spend most of their lives lying in wait at the bottom of their stretch of wetland.

Snappers are predators and take large numbers of fish, waterfowl and even other reptiles. Surprisingly they also eat vegetation, and where houses border on marshes they may well pay gardens a visit. Ripe tomatoes are a favourite food.

They are Ontario's largest turtle, and should a fisherman hook one by accident, he will likely think he has hooked onto a good-sized chunk of driftwood — until he sees what's on the other end of his line! Unhooking one of these creatures without harming it or yourself is a difficult task. It is no fun sharing a small boat with 50 or so pounds of enraged snapping turtle.

These turtles were once abundant in lakes in the Lindsay area, but have recently declined thanks to unlimited trapping. I am told that they are popular south of the border as the main ingredient in snapping turtle soup. Restrictions are now in place covering the number of turtles that may be caught. Hopefully these turtles will recover rapidly to their former numbers.

Snapping turtles are seen only rarely out of the water. This one is sunning itself on a cool June day.

Ontario Fish

Fishing is a popular sport in Ontario and the Ministry of Natural Resources, along with a variety of other organizations, is always trying to improve the sport fishing opportunities within the province. Thanks to these efforts, the fishing here is getting better and more accessible as the years go on.

Popular game fish include the small- and largemouth bass, muskellunge, walleye, brown trout and more recently salmon. As a wildlife photographer who doesn't specialize in underwater work, I have only rarely photographed these fish. There are two notable exceptions, and they are the salmon and rainbow trout.

Ontario's own native salmon, called the Ontario salmon, has been extinct since the 1800s. As settlers' dams slowed down the flow of rivers, the spawning habitat they needed disappeared and so did the species.

Recently the Ministry began stocking rivers along the southern Great Lakes with western salmon, particularly the coho and chinook species. They also stocked rainbow trout in some areas, with the result that fishermen flocked to these regions for a chance at some good-sized (30 pounds and up) fish.

Photographers benefitted too. The spawning runs of these fish provide spectacular opportunities to see them as they leap over dams. Some areas that are especially good for viewing opportunities include:

Duffins Creek in Whitby, which is just off the 401 at the Church Street exit. It has rainbow trout in the spring and some salmon in the fall.

Bronte Creek in Oakville, which, while it has no dam, is shallow enough to offer good views of the salmon in late fall. Take the Bronte Road exit off the QEW to Highway 2 and then west to the river.

The Beaver River Fishway, right in the town of Thornbury on Highway 26, is excellent in the spring for rainbows, and so is the *Sydenham River*, just a short drive further along in Owen Sound.

Near the town of Alliston are two excellent spots to see rainbows in April. They are the *Earl Rowe Provincial Park Fishway*, in the provincial park west of the town, and the *Nicolston Dam*, just to the east on Highway 89.

Take Highway 401 to Port Hope and exit at Highway 28 south to Molson Street, and west until you see the Corbett Dam on the Ganaraska River. Here, too, you will find rainbow trout in the spring and salmon in the fall.

Other fish that can be seen spawning, though not leaping, include white suckers, walleye and carp. Remember that in all cases these spawning runs are protected, sometimes by closed seasons and other times by closed stretches of water.

It's also interesting to note that all the salmon you see at these spots will die. They have evolved a life cycle of three to five years that begins and ends in the same river. These days their journey starts when the Ministry dumps thousands of fingerlings into the river and they make their way to the Great Lakes, where they spend the next few years growing into large fish. It is expected that one day a 50-pounder will be caught!

A fall or spring flooding carries to the mature fish the scent of its home river, and if it is ready to breed it begins an odyssey that will end in death. Leaving the lakes, they begin to change physically and soon can no longer feed. They exist now for only one reason, to breed.

When and if they reach their spawning beds, they will have gone by scores of fishermen, over dams and up fish ladders. Ministry biologists will capture many, strip their eggs and take the fertilized eggs to hatcheries to insure a future run.

When it's over, the banks of the river will be littered with the bodies of dead and dying fish. These will soon decay and the remains will enrich the ecosystem for their offspring.

Because of the poor quality of many rivers, and also due to the lack of silt-free spawning beds, few salmon actually hatch in the rivers. As better management of pollution improves the river systems, the day may come when that is not the case, but for now it is. Rainbow trout do not suffer the same fate. Although they are close relatives of the salmon, they do not die after breeding and they have been able to breed successfully without much help from humans.

Try taking an April weekend to go see the fish. You will be glad you did!

Small mouth bass are a favourite fish for summer anglers.

A muskellunge contemplates a leopard frog as its next meal.

Rainbow trout may be seen in the spring along several rivers especially in the southern Georgian Bay region of the province.

All salmon will spawn and die.

Camouflage

Bibliography

Banfield, A.W.F. *The Mammals of Canada*. Toronto: University of Toronto Press, 1974.

Boschung, H.T., et al. *The Audubon Society Field Guide to North American Fishes, Whales and Dolphins*. New York: Chanticleer Press, 1983.

Bull, J., and J. Farrand Jr. *The Audubon Society Field Guide to North American Birds (Eastern Region)*. New York: Chanticleer Press, 1977.

Carbyn, L.N., ed. *Wolves in Canada and Alaska*, #45 of series. Ottawa: Canadian Wildlife Service, 1983.

Digg, A.I. *Mammals of Ontario*. Waterloo: Otter Press, 1974.

Forsyth, A. *Mammals of the Canadian Wild*. Scarborough: Firefly Books, 1985.

Godfrey, W.E. *The Birds of Canada*. National Museums of Canada Bulletin 203, Ottawa, 1966.

Halls, L.K. *Whitetailed Deer, Ecology and Management*. Harrisburg, PA: Stackpole Books, 1984.

Schmidt, J.L., and D.L. Gilbert. *Big Game of North America*. Harrisburg, PA: Stackpole Books, 1978.

Scott, W.B., and E.J. Crossman. *Freshwater Fishes of Canada*. Government of Canada Bulletin 184, Ottawa, 1973.

Taylor, J.D. *Game Animals of North America*. Toronto: Key Porter Books, 1988.

Whitaker, J.O., Jr. *The Audubon Society Field Guide of North American Mammals*. New York: Chanticleer Press, 1980.

The reader may also want to refer to the following publications available from the Ministry of Natural Resources:

Cuming, H.G. *The Moose in Ontario*. (1972)

Kolenosky, G.B., D.R. Voight and R.O. Standfield. *Wolves and Coyotes in Ontario*. (1978)

Quinn, N. *The Lynx*. (1984)

Smith, H.L., and P.L. Verkruysse. *The Whitetailed Deer in Ontario*. (1983)

Magazines which deal with Ontario wildlife include:

Ontario Out of Doors

Seasons (Federation of Ontario Naturalists)

Landmarks (Ministry of Natural Resources)

Conservation Groups in Ontario

If you'd like more information on conservation groups in Ontario, you may wish to contact some of these organizations.

Ministry of Natural Resources
Whitney Block, Queen's Park
99 Wellesley St.
Toronto, Ontario
M7A 1W3

General Inquiries: (416) 965-2000
Fishing: (416) 965-7883
Wildlife: (416) 965-4251
Provincial Parks: (416) 965-3081

Canadian Nature Federation
453 Sussex Drive
Ottawa, Ontario
K1N 6Z4
(613) 238-6154

Ducks Unlimited
240 Bayview Ave.
Barrie, Ontario
L4M 3B3
(705) 726-3825

Ontario Federation of Anglers and Hunters
Box 28, 169 Charlotte Street
Peterborough, Ontario
K9J 6Y5
(705) 748-6324

Federation of Ontario Naturalists
355 Lesmill Road
Don Mills, Ontario
M3B 2W8
(416) 444-8419

Elk

Index